"Simon wants his food to make you smile. And I've no doubt it will."

FOREWORD

DANIEL CLIFFORD – CHEF PATRON, MIDSUMMER HOUSE

==

When I signed up to become one of the judges on the new series of *Celebrity MasterChef Ireland*, I was excited about the prospect of meeting people who were at various levels of culinary expertise. What I looked forward to most was getting involved with each of the contestants and helping them become better cooks – and having some fun along the way.

With Simon, I got both. The first time we met was in the first round of the competition: a nervous moment for him and his fellow competitors. But straight away his sense of humour was evident. When the contestants were asked to put their *MasterChef* aprons on for the first time and Simon was clearly struggling getting it tied, he quickly quipped, 'I think this is your size, Nadia'. For those that don't know, Nadia Forde, who was great company during the show, is a multi-talented, stunning actress/model, who could make any outfit look good! The rest of the contestants laughed, as did myself and my fellow judge Robin Gill. Simon had managed to turn a very tense moment for all involved into a light-hearted one. He managed to put the other contestants at ease, and at the same time introduce himself to the show.

From that moment on, Simon continued to keep the kitchen laughing all the way up to the final, where he found himself cooking at a level he never thought possible. What impressed me most about Simon was his passion for food, which I could clearly see right from the start. When he undercooked his lamb in the first round, I could see from his face that Simon was gutted, but, typical Simon, he said, 'When I took the lamb out of the oven it was so cold the lamb said, "Put me back in, I'm freezing."'

He went on to cook some of the best dishes in the entire series, including his ostrich pie (which he promised to give me the recipe for!), his risotto (which won the critics' round) and, of course, that pork dish in the final, which was amazing. He grew during the process, in confidence, and as a cook, and that shone through in the semi-final of the competition, when he was faced with the busiest section in the kitchen in the once-Michelin-star restaurant Picd à Terre in London. As I said on the day, 'He smashed it. He was like a man possessed.'

During the competition I got to know Simon a little better, and I told him that he reminded me of the man who runs our front-of-house in Midsummer House, Jean-François Imbert. Men of similar deportment, Simon and Jean-François are also both performers, entertainers. They treat the kitchen as theatre. No matter what their day has brought them, when service starts, it's showtime. That excites me. And so does Simon's first cookbook. He's taken a genre of cooking, home-style American diner food, and put his own mark on it. In these recipes, you can feel Simon's passion for the ingredients and the food. Most importantly, you can tell he's cooking them for you. He wants his food to make you smile. And I've no doubt it will.

I'm looking forward to seeing Simon continue to grow as a cook, and to taste the results. Whoever goes on this journey with him will do so laughing all the way!

Daniel Clifford

Born in Canterbury, Kent, in 1973, Daniel spent the first twelve years of his career training in some of the best restaurants in the UK and France. Jean Bardet in France, whom Daniel cites as his biggest influence, Simon Gueller at Rascasse and Marco Pierre White at The Box Tree have all contributed to Daniel's development into one of the country's most respected chefs.

Daniel's menu and style of food focuses on the most seasonal produce and his dishes are developed to make the taste as natural as possible.

The MENU

BREAKFAST

- Buttermilk Pancakes with Crispy Bacon and Maple Syrup   15
- Huevos Rancheros   17
- Corned Beef Hash, with Home Fries and 2 Eggs (Sunny Side Up!)   20
- New York Açai Bowl   23
- Eggs Benedict with Chorizo Patties   27
- Pastrami and Potato Tortilla   29
- French Toast with Cinnamon, Pecans and Strawberries   31
- Granola and Yoghurt Pots   32
- Fried Green Tomatoes *(not from the Whistle Stop Café!)*   34
- Chinese Cha Siu Pork Buns   36

APPETISERS

- Split Pea and Ham Hock Soup   47
- Matzo Ball Soup with Pulled Chicken   52
- Crab Cakes with Butter Sauce   54
- Fried Calamari with Sweet Chilli Sauce   55
- Sticky Baked Buffalo Wings, Dublin-Style   57
- Crispy Duck Salad   59
- Classic Caesar Salad   60
- Californian Cobb Salad Wrap   62
- Mardi Gras Prawn Cocktail   65
- Roast Ear of Corn with Coriander Chophouse Butter   67

MAINS

SANDWICHES

DESSERTS

COCKTAILS

SIDES

OVEN TEMPERATURES

All of the temperatures in the recipes are for a fan assisted oven, so a slight adjustment may be needed if you are using a non-fan assisted oven!

INTRODUCTION

A cookbook. Who'd have thought it?

I've been a freelance actor, writer, director, presenter and producer for almost twenty years. During that time I've put pen to paper and written various things: pitches for TV comedies and dramas, feature-film scripts, documentaries, TV and radio commercials, I've even started work on a novel. Something I never thought I'd write was a cookbook. And yet here we are.

My journey with food, like most people's, started at home. My mother was a great cook, not flamboyant, but she cooked the kind of meals that we are all familiar with: those one-pot wonders filled with ingredients that made it in through necessity rather than invention. Good, basic, home-cooked food. It's still my favourite type of cuisine. I wasn't one of those kids that stood beside my mother and watched how she cooked in an attempt to learn; I had no interest in cooking, so I didn't pull up a stool beside her and get involved enthusiastically. I was the child that pulled a chair up to the table, banged my fork on that table and shouted, 'Is it ready yet?' repeatedly until the meal was placed in front of me. I've a couple of kids of that type at home now myself. I do, however, remember certain dishes that my mother made. Stews,

casseroles, roasts. Mammy dinners. Those are the types of dishes I now cook regularly at home. I guess I learned how to cook from her subliminally. I was always in my mother's pocket, always at her feet, so I suppose all that time I spent at her side (normally pulling at her leg, demanding attention) paid off in culinary terms.

My mother passed away when I was nineteen, and my dad just seven years later, so at the age of twenty-six I had to learn how to feed myself. I was lucky that both of my sisters Sarah and Debbie could, and still can, cook brilliantly.

My brother Dave, bless him, struggles on the cooking front. I have tried over the years to make it my mission to teach him. I remember at one point going over to his house to show him how to make spaghetti bolognese. It took us about two hours, and we ate the results, but I still think to this day if I asked him to make one he'd ring my sister and ask her for help.

But one thing I loved doing in those years at home, when just the four of us were there, was cooking for my brother and sisters. I still do it to this day. I love having them over and feeding them. I'm a feeder. We make our version of home-made pizzas. Dave's son Denis loves the whole palaver of rolling out the dough, putting his favourite toppings on, and then watching the clock on the oven as he counts down the seven minutes it takes for them to cook. My brother will stand there and watch, and ask the same question when I put the finished pizza down in front of him: 'Jaysus, that's lovely, how do make it again?' My own boys, Cameron, Elliot, Isaac and Lewis, all love the home-made pizzas – well maybe not Lewis, he's still only got six teeth – but you know what I mean! That's what I get out of cooking: putting a smile on people's faces as they tuck into whatever you've made.

A strong food memory for me as a child is Christmas. My mam loved Christmas, as do I. She loved the build-up, the presents, Santa, making the Christmas cake and so on, but especially the Christmas dinner: the turkey and ham, with all the trimmings, followed by a trifle. But most of all, it was the meal we had on Christmas mornings that I remember the best. Coddle. Yep, a bowl of delicious Dublin coddle. For those of you not familiar with it, it's basically a clear stew, and everybody's version of it is different. My mother's had sausages, bacon rashers (cut into bite-size pieces), and an onion. If my grandmother (she was from Derry originally) came over, she would add barley, which is an old-fashioned ingredient that was used in a coddle. My wife, Lisa, and I have our version of coddle, which has all of the above, minus the barley (sorry, Nana). We add potatoes, and we use ham pieces and bacon ribs. Delish. To this very day, my sisters cook a coddle every Christmas morning as a nod to our mam and dad and Christmases past. Any time I smell a coddle cooking, it immediately transports me back to Christmas morning.

My dad wasn't what you'd call handy around the kitchen. He'd put a shelf up for you, which usually fell down within three weeks (DIY wasn't his thing either), but he wouldn't get involved in the cooking. I guess it was a generational thing. My mam cooked; he ate. And his food tastes were very simple: a pork chop and spuds, a stew, fish and chips. Meals of their time. Good meals, but nothing adventurous. I don't think my father ever ate spaghetti or rice. In fact, the mention of them would be greeted with disdain. 'Not for me, thanks' was the look you'd get if you suggested that for a potential dinner on a Wednesday. However, he did have some peculiar tastes. He had a fondness for tripe, brawn and lap of mutton.

In the first round of *Celebrity MasterChef*, we were asked to cook a dish that reminded us of our childhood, and I went with a dish that reminded me of both my mam and dad. We lived in a very normal terraced three-bed house, and on one side of us were our neighbours, the Cullens. They were great neighbours. Even though we lived on the suburban Northside of Dublin, the Cullens had a farm in Roundwood, Co. Wicklow. It was their family farm, and most weekends they would head down there, work the farm and return to Dublin on a Sunday night. One of my earliest memories is standing in the kitchen with my mam, never far from her side, looking out the kitchen window and waiting, and waiting. Then we'd see it: a plastic bag, filled with meat, sailing over the wall from the Cullens, into our back garden. Me or my brother would be dispatched to fetch the bag, which would contain various cuts of meat, normally lamb, that Betty (always 'Mrs Cullen' to me) would bring home from the farm for my mam. My mam would then cook the contents over the following week, to my father's delight,

because as I've said, one of his favourite meals was lap of mutton – a very fatty piece of meat. And he would like it curried. Yes, curried. But that's not all, oh no. A few days after the lap-of-mutton curry was finished, whatever meat was left over went into a sandwich. 'Waste not, want not' and all of that. Ah yes, a cold, curried lap-of-mutton sandwich. That recipe, I can assure you, has not made the final cut here. Sorry, Dad.

I do have a strong memory of my dad cooking one thing: boiled eggs. It was his morning ritual after my mam passed away. It was almost ceremonial. Laid out on the table were the tea towel (to capture any crumbs), the egg cups (which were as old as he was), the two pieces of toast (cut into soldiers) and the cup of tea. A meal fit for a king. Our king.

In fairness to my dad, I wasn't the most adventurous of eaters either. It wasn't until I met Lisa that I developed a wider appreciation of ingredients. I wasn't a big fan of vegetables. A tin of peas was as far as I'd go. But when we started living together, Lisa encouraged me to try them, and slowly I've grown to love my veg, to the point where my wife and my sisters slag me, saying, 'Everything he cooks has a leek in it.'

My food tastes moved on as I started to travel around the world through my job. I found myself in places like Bulgaria, eating wild boar served on a wooden board in a pub; in Poland, where we feasted on lots of types of sauerkraut; and in Russia, where I don't remember much, because every meal we had was accompanied by copious amounts of vodka. But I found the food I love most when I first arrived in the home of the Stars and Stripes: America. There I not only found food that appealed to my 'home-cooking' palate, but also portions that blew me away.

Daniel Clifford with Simon during Celebrity Masterchef

I've been lucky to film right across the US, from New York to Dallas to Los Angeles. And whenever I was there working, I found myself spending more and more time in my favourite type of eatery: the diner. The classic American diner. I love them. I love the diner vibe. Because while I'm away working, I'm travelling alone, so I'll spend my time in a diner, reading or writing, tucking into a classic turkey burger and constantly aware of the activity around me. The different types of conversations you overhear, from the Wall Street types talking about finance in New York, to the wannabe writers and actors discussing scripts in LA, to the Texans discussing the heat and how it will affect their crops, there's always a buzz. From the decor to the service, from the variety of dishes on the menus to the array of characters that inhabit them, I've fallen in love with the classic American diner.

If you haven't already seen it, watch the opening sequence from my favourite Woody Allen movie, *Broadway Danny Rose*. The camera tracks through a busy NYC diner; we pass waiters, trays of food, all types of customers, businessmen, truck drivers. You hear the sounds of the diner, and by the time the camera settles on our hero's table, you can almost taste the cheeseburgers.

Myself and my good pal John Carney (who wrote and directed *Once* and *Sing Street*) have been friends since we shot *Bachelors Walk* together all those years ago. We share similar passions. Frank Sinatra. New York. Woody Allen. And diners. On a trip to NYC a few years ago, when we were both there working on separate projects, John called me one night and said (in a spot-on New York accent), 'You wanna go to the Carnegie and grab a sandwich?' He was talking about the Carnegie Deli, one of NYC's most famous food landmarks (sadly now closed). We met, sat at a small table in the crowded diner, and I ordered my sandwich, the 'Broadway Danny Rose'. What a sandwich. What a night. John, being John, filmed the entire experience. It's on YouTube, titled *Me and Simon grab a sandwich in New York*. Look it up and you'll see what I mean about the 'diner vibe'.

But of course, it's the food that brings me through the doors of the diner time after time. Whether I'm there eating breakfast, grabbing a quick deli-style sandwich on the run, tucking into a hearty lunch of meat loaf, grabbing a slice of Key lime pie as an afternoon treat, or meeting friends and colleagues over a feast of ribs for dinner, what amazes me most is the variety of dishes that are on offer.

My food journey came to a crescendo when I was asked to take part in the latest series of *Celebrity MasterChef Ireland*. What an experience. Right from the first day, when we cooked our 'childhood memory' dish, through our first service in a professional kitchen in Charlotte Quay, the masterclasses with Claire Clark, cooking for the critics, the service in Pied à Terre in London, right the way to the final, I relished every single minute of the process. I met some amazing people on the show, great characters: Mundy, Oisín McConville, Niamh Kavanagh, Evelyn Cusack, Sonia O'Sullivan, Holly Carpenter, Mumbalicious (Samantha Mumba), Nadia Forde and Colm O'Gorman. Great people, and great cooks. The competition was stressful, exhausting, exciting, nerve-jangling, fierce. Myself, Niamh and Oisín made it to the final, with Niamh coming out on top as the champion, and I couldn't have been happier for her. As we say in Dublin, she's 'a darlin' woman', and a damn fine cook!

Guiding us through the show were our two judges, Robin Gill and Daniel Clifford, both amazing chefs at the top of their game. They were incredible to work with and it was a privilege to watch them cook in their masterclasses. They gave us invaluable advice and help, became invested in us, and wanted to watch us grow as cooks, which we inevitably did. They are friends for life.

I approached *MasterChef* as I did every other job: be professional, do your best, don't let yourself down and, above all, have fun doing it. I was extremely proud of what we *all* achieved on that series. The people behind the show, the entire team at Shinawil productions, did an unbelievable job, particularly Niamh Maher and Ailbhe Maher, our producers, who supported us all the way through. To them, I owe huge thanks.

And so to this, my first cookbook. As I said earlier, who'd have thought it? Honestly? I did! As soon as I finished my journey on *MasterChef*, I thought 'Why not?' and when it came to picking a theme for the book, what type of cooking I'd like to write about, the answer was obvious to me: the classic American diner. The food I love.

During *MasterChef*, I leaned on another friend, Neal Kearns (Executive Head Chef at the Castleknock Hotel and Country Club). He opened his kitchen to me, and his culinary brain. He guided me through my ideas for dishes in the competition, told me where I was going wrong, trained me, pushed me. Naturally I turned to Neal when I was thinking of doing a cookbook. Straightaway he was on

board. We got stuck in, coming up with dishes and recipes, and this book is the end result. Neal, you're a diamond. (See what I did there?)

What I've done in this book is take some of the world's favourite diner dishes and adapt them for the home cook. I've always wanted to learn how to replicate my favourite diner dishes at home, and what I want to do with this book is give you the chance to do the same. The experience I want to give you, the reader, is that diner experience. I've laid the book out like a diner menu, so feel free to browse through it, have a starter, go straight for a main, dive into a delicious dessert, or, if the mood takes you, pick something from the breakfast menu. That's what I love about diners: day or night, summer or winter, you can have your favourite comfort food dish whenever you want it.

My favourite thing to do in a diner is to order my favourite breakfast dish (corned beef hash, home fries and two eggs sunny side up) at midnight, or order a Reuben sandwich at 7 a.m. That's what a diner offers: choice. Whatever you want, whenever you want it.

So, have a browse through my diner menu, pick your favourite dish and tuck in. And don't worry about what time of day it is. No one here is judging you. Enjoy!

Order up!

BREAKFAST

"Ask not what you can do for your country. Ask what's for lunch."

— ORSON WELLES

"I always cook with wine. Sometimes I even add it to the food."

— W.C FIELDS

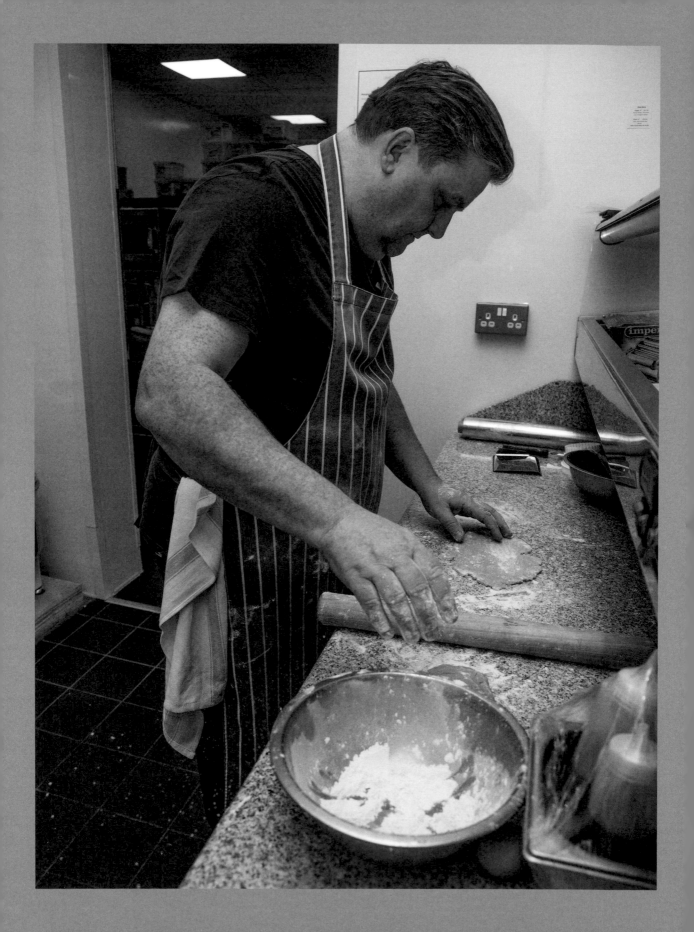

My first experience of diner food in the US was breakfast. Having got off a plane the night before and enjoyed the local hospitality a little too much, the following morning I was brought to a diner in Yonkers. As soon as the door opened, I knew I was in for a good feed. In fact, I felt at home. The place was bustling, there were waitresses dashing around the room, the smell of bacon on the grill, stacks of pancakes on the tables where hungry customers tucked in, and the smell of freshly ground coffee. This place was everything I'd imagined it would be. Heaven, with bacon.

In this chapter, I've tried to offer you a variety of dishes, all diner classics, and all to suit different tastes and levels of hunger!

For the health-conscious amongst you (thank you for buying this book: you complete me) there are the delicious granola and yoghurt pots and the New York-style açai bowl. For those of you who like your breakfast stacked high, tuck into the pancakes and maple syrup, or the Chinese Cha Siu pork buns. Staying on the lighter side of lunch, there's the French toast served with pecans and strawberries, but if you feeling that little bit hungrier, go for the pastrami and potato tortilla: I guarantee this will set you up for the day! If, like me, you like a little taste of home mixed with the good old U. S. of A., then there's the corned beef hash with home fries and two eggs – sunny side up, of course.

BUTTERMILK PANCAKES

WITH CRISPY BACON AND MAPLE SYRUP

● ●

This dish is an absolute staple on every diner menu from Cape May, New Jersey, to Fresno, California. It's also Mrs Delaney's go-to diner breakfast dish. She doesn't even bother looking at the menu any more. It's one of the most popular dishes on a diner's breakfast menu, and I think it's because of the contrasts of flavours and textures on the plate. You start with the soft, fluffy buttermilk pancakes, and then crunch through that crispy bacon, all topped off with that silky maple sauce. Hungry? Let's get cooking . . .

SERVES 4

- 225 G PLAIN FLOUR
- 2 TBSP CASTER SUGAR
- 1 TSP BICARBONATE OF SODA
- 2 FREE-RANGE EGGS
- 300 ML BUTTERMILK
- 50 ML MILK
- 50 G BUTTER, MELTED
- 1 TSP SALT
- 3 TBSP RAPESEED OIL, FOR FRYING
- 8 SLICES SMOKED STREAKY BACON
  OR PANCETTA
- 2 TBSP SOFT BROWN SUGAR
- KNOB OF BUTTER, TO SERVE

Sieve the flour, caster sugar and bicarbonate of soda into a bowl. Separate the eggs: put the whites into another bowl, and add the yolks the flour mixture.

Add the buttermilk, milk and melted butter to the flour mix, and mix well. Don't worry about leaving a few small lumps, this isn't *MasterChef*, and it gives the pancakes a nice lift. Whisk the egg whites with the salt until you have stiff peaks. Gently fold the egg-white mix into the batter. Heat a frying pan and brush with a little oil (I like to use rapeseed oil).

Add a ladle of batter to the pan (should be the size of the palm of your hand) and cook until you start to see small bubbles dimple the top of the pancake. When you see the bubbles, flip. Cook for another 30 seconds, until golden, and then remove the pan from the heat and set aside the pancake. Repeat until all the batter is used.

Throw a tea towel over the pancakes to keep them warm. This recipe should get you about 12 in total.

BUTTERMILK PANCAKES

Now the bacon: sprinkle the slices with the brown sugar (not too much) before frying, then place them in a hot pan and cook until crispy.

To serve, stack the pancakes (as many as you dare!) and put the crispy bacon on top, drizzle with maple syrup and, for an extra sneaky treat, add a little knob of butter over the top.

This recipe has been approved by Mrs Delaney.

HUEVOS RANCHEROS

●●●

This dish originated as a large mid morning meal on rural farms in Mexico. It's another diner breakfast staple, and it's one of those dishes that you can put your own slant on. You can add a side of refried beans or guacamole; it depends on how hungry you are! My recipe uses shop-bought tortillas. You can of course make your own, but in this day and age the quality of the shop-bought ones is so good. And when time is not your friend, these work perfectly. Adding a warm salsa gives this dish that mix of textures and flavours that I love, and of course I have an Irish slant, using a good Irish Cheddar. This dish is spicy, warm and comforting: the perfect pick-me-up.

SERVES 4

- OLIVE OIL, FOR FRYING
- 1 RED ONION, FINELY CHOPPED
- 1 GARLIC CLOVE, CRUSHED
- 3 RIPE TOMATOES, DESEEDED AND FINELY CHOPPED
- 1 TSP GRANULATED SUGAR
- 1 JALAPEÑO PEPPER, FINELY CHOPPED
- 4 TORTILLAS, 9 INCHES WIDE
- 8 FREE RANGE EGGS
- 50 G FRESH CORIANDER
- 1 AVOCADO
- 100 G WHITE IRISH CHEDDAR, GRATED
- 1 LIME
- SALT AND PEPPER, TO SEASON

Start with the salsa. Heat a small pan to a medium heat, add a little olive oil and the finely chopped onion. Allow to cook gently until soft and with a little colour. Add the garlic, chopped tomato, sugar and jalapeño, and cook gently for about ten minutes.

In a large frying pan, heat a touch of oil on a medium heat. Once hot, toast the tortilla (I like the edges to crisp a little). Once toasted, cover them with a tea towel to keep warm. Then, in the same pan, fry the eggs until soft.

To serve, add the coriander to the salsa and slice the avocado. Place a tortilla on a plate and 2 eggs per person on top, add the cheese and the avocado, and then spoon over your warm salsa, squeeze some lime juice over, season with salt and pepper and dig in.

"There is one thing more exasperating than a wife who can cook and won't, and that's a wife who can't cook and will."

— ROBERT FROST

"The only time to eat diet food is while you're waiting for the steak to cook."

— JULIA CHILD

CORNED BEEF HASH

WITH HOME FRIES AND TWO EGGS

●●●

The first time I set foot in the States, nearly 20 years ago, in New York City, I was staying with friends up in Yonkers, an Irish foothold about twenty-five minutes upstate on the train from Grand Central. On my first morning there, a little worse for wear (it must have been the jet lag, not the copious amounts of beer consumed on my first night in the Big Apple), I was brought by my old pal Michelle to a diner called Eileen's Country Kitchen. An Irish diner. 'Wow,' I thought, 'I can get stuck into a full Irish.' Not a bit of it. I spotted corned beef hash on the menu. I asked Michelle what it was. 'Pulled corned beef served with crispy potatoes and topped off with two fried eggs,' she told me. I was sold. My love affair with this dish started then, and honestly, this dish started my love affair with diners in general.

As recently as eighteen months ago, back in NYC while staying with Michelle's brother Cathal, we went into Eileen's for our breakfast. I didn't even pick the menu up. 'Let me guess,' Cathal said in his Dublin brogue (even though he's been there for thirty years!), 'you're going for the corned beef hash.'

'Spot on,' I replied.

'Some things never change,' he said as he ordered his daily bowl of porridge.

This dish brings a smile to my face every time I order it. And now, I love to cook it. And I'd love you to try it too . . .

SERVES 4-6

FOR THE DINER-STYLE HOME FRIES:
· 3 MEDIUM ROOSTER OR MARIS PIPER POTATOES
· 2 TBSP RAPESEED OIL
· 50 G UNSALTED BUTTER
· 1 MEDIUM ONION, FINELY DICED
· ½ TSP GARLIC POWDER
· ½ TSP SMOKED PAPRIKA
· ½ TSP JAMAICAN JERK SPICE
· SALT AND PEPPER, TO SEASON
· 50 G FRESH PARSLEY, FINELY CHOPPED

FOR THE CORNED BEEF HASH:
· 2 TBSP RAPESEED OIL
· 240 G CORNED BEEF, SHREDDED (SEE SIDES, P. 210)
· 2 MEDIUM ROOSTER OR MARIS PIPER POTATOES
· 1 MEDIUM ONION, FINELY CHOPPED
· 4 LARGE FREE-RANGE EGGS
· 100 G RICH CHEDDAR CHEESE, GRATED
· SALT AND PEPPER, TO SEASON

Start with the home fries. Dice the potatoes (leaving the skin on) into bite-size pieces. Put them into a large saucepan of cold water, add a pinch of salt, bring to the boil, then simmer for 8-10 minutes until the potatoes are almost cooked. Strain them and set aside. In a frying pan heat one tablespoon of the oil with the butter over a medium heat, and add the onions and spices. Cook for about 7 minutes, or until the onions are soft. Add your parboiled potatoes to the pan and cook on a high heat until nice and golden (normally takes about 8 minutes).

On to the hash itself. In another frying pan, heat 2 tablespoons of the oil and add the shredded corned beef and cook for about two minutes (you really just want to heat the meat through). Grate the two potatoes, pop them into a towel and squeeze the excess water from them. Add the potatoes to the pan along with the finely chopped onion. Mix well and allow to cook gently, without stirring, for about 6 minutes. When cooked, place a plate on top on top of the pan and, using a tea towel, turn the pan over so the mixture is now on the plate. Put the mix back into the pan and cook for a further 10 minutes. In another pan, fry your four eggs in a little oil, and for sunny side up just cook without flipping the eggs. Just before serving the hash, add the grated cheese to the top of the mix and allow it to melt a little.

To serve, portion the hash onto a plate, place your eggs on top, and add the home fries on the side. To garnish the home fries, add a little finely chopped parsley before you serve.

THE NEW YORK-STYLE AÇAI BOWL

●●●

The açai berry, pronounced aaahhsüügghhhyeeee, has come to the forefront of food fads over the past couple of years. But, unlike most, it seems to be here to stay. This superfood, all the way from Brazil, has found its way into the bowls of millions of breakfasts around the world for those who want a healthy start to their day. But, and I'm being honest here, unlike most superfoods, the best thing about this little berry, apart from all its health benefits, is its taste. This recipe uses açai berry powder, which is made from freeze-dried açai berries, as it's easier to get your hands on than the berries or the berry purée itself! A great way to start your day, and you can add the fruits of your choice to the bowl. It's your call!

SERVES 4

FOR THE AÇAI MIX:
- 100 G AÇAI POWDER (CAN BE BOUGHT EASILY IN ANY GOOD HEALTH FOOD SHOP)
- 500 G FROZEN BERRIES (CHOOSE YOUR FAVOURITES HERE, A MIXTURE IS ALWAYS GOOD!)
- 250 ML MILK, OR YOUR FAVOURITE KIND OF JUICE: WHICHEVER YOU PREFER
- 1 TSP HONEY

FOR THE TOPPINGS:
THESE CAN BE ANYTHING YOU WANT! CHOOSE YOUR FAVOURITES. THESE ARE AMONG MINE:
- SLICED BANANA
- DRIED APRICOTS AND FRUITS
- SEEDS, LIKE CHIA AND SUNFLOWER ETC.
- FRESH BERRIES, LIKE BLUEBERRIES, RASPBERRIES ETC.
- GRANOLA (OPTIONAL)

Make the thick açai base by blending all the ingredients together (apart from the toppings) until smooth. Follow the instructions on the pack of açai powder. You want it to be the consistency of a nice bowl of porridge, but if it's too thick, add a little milk or juice to thin it out. Pour into a serving bowl.

Then add your favourite toppings. You could add some granola if you want. Couldn't be easier.

EGGS BENEDICT

WITH CHORIZO PATTIES AND HOLLANDAISE SAUCE

●●●

There are lots of stories about where this dish originated, but this is my favourite: in 1894, Lemuel Benedict, a Wall Street broker who was suffering from a hangover, ordered 'some buttered toast, crisp bacon, two poached eggs, and a hooker of hollandaise sauce' at the Waldorf Hotel in New York. The Waldorf's legendary chef, Oscar Tschirky, was so impressed that he put the dish on his breakfast and luncheon menus after substituting Canadian bacon for crisp bacon and a toasted English muffin for toasted bread.

One of the most ordered dishes in diner history is eggs Benny, and it's another one of those dishes that has as many variations as there are stars in the sky. That's what I love about eating in different diners in different parts of the US: every diner's eggs Benny is different. With my recipe I've added a little twist: I've used a chorizo patty instead of the ham that's usually served. And hey, if you haven't the time and the patience to make your own hollandaise, a shop-bought one will be fine. But if you do make the effort, you'll thank me!

SERVES 4

FOR THE HOLLANDAISE:
- 2 EGG YOLKS
- 1 TSP LEMON JUICE
- 1 TSP WHITE WINE VINEGAR
- 115 G UNSALTED BUTTER, MELTED

FOR THE POACHED EGGS:
- WHITE WINE VINEGAR
- 8 EGGS

FOR THE CHORIZO PATTIES:
- 200 G PORK SAUSAGE MEAT
- 200 G CHORIZO SAUSAGE MEAT
- OLIVE OIL, FOR FRYING

So, let's start with the hollandaise. Bring a saucepan of water to the boil and as soon as it does, kill the heat. Grab a large bowl and pop in the egg yolks, whisk them up with the lemon juice and the white wine vinegar until you really start to see the mixture thicken. Put the bowl over the saucepan of hot water and slowly pour in the melted butter as you continue to whisk constantly to form what's called an emulsion, which should be a little thinner than a mayonnaise. Leave the bowl sitting on the pan when done, ready to serve, and don't panic if the mixture thickens up a little: just add a drop of hot water to thin it out again.

So, on to the poached eggs. In a large pot, boil some water, and then turn it down to a simmer. Add a little drop of white wine vinegar and then carefully break the eggs into the water. (It's easier if you crack the egg into a small cup and drop it into the water: it stops

EGGS BENEDICT

TO SERVE:
· 4 ENGLISH MUFFINS, OR THE BREAD OF YOUR CHOICE
· 110 G BUTTER
· PINCH OF CAYENNE PEPPER

the egg white from going all over the pot.) Cook until the egg is set – in other words, no longer transparent, but before it goes hard – then remove the egg with a slotted spoon and leave to sit on some kitchen paper. (During *MasterChef*, Daniel Clifford showed me the twice-cooked method. Drop the eggs into the water for a minute, then take them out, and just before you serve, give them another minute in the hot water. Easy peasy. Believe me, if I can do it, you can!)

On to the chorizo patties. Skin all of the sausages, both the pork ones and the chorizo ones, and put them in a bowl and mix them so they form one mixture. Then shape them into small patties, as flat as you can, as they'll cook quicker and more evenly. In a small pan, heat a little olive oil, and lay the patties in, two per portion. Cook until coloured, then flip over and fry until cooked through, which should take 7–8 minutes.

To serve, toast the English muffins, spread a little of the melted butter on them, and place on your serving plate. Add the chorizo patties on top, then the poached eggs, and dress with the hollandaise. Sprinkle a little cayenne pepper over the sauce. Serve these with home fries (see p. 20) and, baby, you'll be in NYC in a heartbeat!

PASTRAMI AND POTATO TORTILLA

This dish is a nod to our Spanish friends, and it features heavily in tapas bars all over their beautiful country. It's found its way onto diner menus and onto the home dinner table because of its versatility. You can add or take away whatever ingredients take your fancy. You can change the main event too, the pastrami, to whatever meat you like, or remove it altogether and you've got a cracking vegetarian dish.

SERVES 4

- 5 ROOSTER POTATOES, THINLY SLICED
- 1 WHITE ONION, THINLY SLICED
- 3 TBSP OLIVE OIL
- 200 G PASTRAMI, DICED
- 6 FREE-RANGE EGGS
- 340 ML CREAM
- A HANDFUL OF IRISH WHITE CHEDDAR, GRATED
- A HANDFUL OF PARMESAN, GRATED
- 2 LARGE SPRING ONIONS, SLICED
- SALT AND PEPPER TO TASTE

As with most Irish meals, let's start with the spuds. Peel and finely slice your potatoes, not wafer thin, but thin enough that they will cook in about 8 minutes. Pop these into a pot of salted boiling water and cook until nice and tender. Then drain them and set aside.

In a pan, add half of the olive oil, and on a medium heat pop in your sliced onions and cook for a couple of minutes until soft. Add in your pastrami and cook for another few minutes until the pastrami is nice and crisp. When the onions and pastrami are good to go, take them out of the pan and set aside.

In a bowl, beat the eggs, cream and a little salt and pepper together. Add in the cheeses and the chopped scallions, and the onion and pastrami mix.

Add another drop of oil to your pan, heat, and pour in the eggs and spuds mixture. Cook on a low heat until the tortilla is a golden colour and set: this should take around 10 minutes. To flip, place a plate over the pan, carefully turn it over and then return the tortilla to the pan and finish cooking for another 5 or 6 minutes. To serve, cut a nice slice, pop on a plate and serve with a crunchy green salad. A ranch dressing (see p. 207) goes brilliantly with this.

FRENCH TOAST

WITH CINNAMON, PECANS AND STRAWBERRIES

●●●

This is a quick and easy breakfast dish to make. It's also a great way to get the kids eating more fruit. Choose whatever berries are in season and take your fancy; don't be afraid to mix up. I'm using strawberries because I'd eat them all day every day if I could. In this recipe I'm using a sliced fruit loaf, which can be bought in any good supermarket or delicatessen. This fruit loaf has pecans and seeds in it, but, again, go for your favoured bread and tuck in . . .

SERVES 4

· 300 G FRUIT LOAF
· 4 FREE-RANGE EGGS
· 70 ML MILK
· 70 ML CREAM
· 3 DROPS NATURAL VANILLA EXTRACT
· ½ TSP GROUND CINNAMON
· PINCH OF SALT
· 2 TSP SUGAR
· 250 G STRAWBERRIES, AND A HANDFUL EXTRA FOR DECORATION
· 40 G BUTTER
· ICING SUGAR (FOR DECORATION)
· MAPLE SYRUP (OPTIONAL)

Simplicity itself. Start with a large bowl, and add all the ingredients except the butter and the fruit loaf, and whisk with a fork until well combined. Simply soak the bread in this mixture for a couple of minutes until the slices are saturated! Then, in a pan, melt the butter, and pop the slices of bread in, two at a time depending on the size of the pan, and cook for about 3 minutes on each side. They should go a lovely golden colour. To serve, stack a couple of slices of the bread on top of each other, adding a handful of sliced strawberries and a dusting of icing sugar on top. If you're feeling devilish, spoon a drop of maple syrup over the bread.

GRANOLA AND YOGHURT POTS

•●•

A lot of us don't have the luxury of time in the mornings to prepare a diner-style breakfast, but this recipe is not only quick and easy to make, it's also a healthy option and one that the kids will go for too. Get them involved in making the pots, choosing their favourite fruits and toppings. You can pop this breakfast into a sealable tub or pot and send them off to school with it, or pop one into your laptop bag and you've got a tasty, healthy lunch ready to go. It's also a recipe where you can make a large batch and it will keep for weeks. What I love about this dish is that you can tailor it to include all of your favourite types of seeds, fruits and toppings.

- 100 G DRIED CRANBERRIES
- 100 G DRIED APRICOTS
- 200 G PORRIDGE OATS
- 35 G SESAME SEEDS
- 50 G SUNFLOWER SEEDS
- 100 G GOJI BERRIES
- ½ TSP SALT
- 200 G ORGANIC HONEY
- 1 TBSP SOFT BROWN SUGAR
- 1 VANILLA POD, DESEEDED
- 1 POT OF NATURAL YOGHURT

Preheat your oven to 140°C.

Chop the cranberries, goji berries and apricots and mix with the rest of the dry ingredients. In a small pan, gently heat the honey, sugar and vanilla seeds. When the sugar has dissolved, quickly add the wet ingredients to the dried and mix thoroughly. Spread the mix onto a baking tray that is lined with a sheet of silicone paper. Place on the middle shelf of the oven and bake for 40 minutes, checking that the mix is not browning too quickly. If it is, just lower the temperature. Remove from oven and allow to cool. Once cool, store in an airtight container for up to 3 weeks.

Serve with a dollop of natural yoghurt, and sprinkle a few of your favourite berries on top.

FRIED GREEN TOMATOES

(NOT FROM THE WHISTLE STOP CAFÉ!)

●●

Contrary to popular opinion, this is a dish that doesn't originate from the Southern states of the US. According to Robert F. Moss, author of The Fried Green Tomato Swindle and Other Culinary Adventures *(yes, there is such a book, Google it!), fried green tomatoes first appear in nineteenth-century Northeastern and Midwestern cookbooks such as the 1877* Buckeye Cookbook. *In fact, the 1919* International Jewish Cookbook *by Florence Kreisler Greenbaum contained 1,600 recipes that explained the rules of koshering (making kosher) from America, Germany, Austria, Russia, France and Poland. The movie that made the dish famous* (Fried Green Tomatoes at the Whistle Stop Café) *got its inspiration from a real café called The Irondale Café, which did serve the dish, but staff there said it didn't feature heavily on the menu – that is, until the movie came out. Thousands have since flocked there to order the dish. I've saved you the plane fare.*

By the way, on the green tomatoes, these might not be available in your supermarket, but pop into any good veg shop and they'll be there. Alternatively, if you can't find them, the more readily available beef tomato will be just as tasty!

SERVES 4

- ½ TSP SMOKED PAPRIKA
- 500 G PLAIN FLOUR
- 1 GARLIC CLOVE, CRUSHED
- 350 ML BUTTERMILK
- 4 LARGE GREEN TOMATOES (OR BEEF TOMATOES)
- 25 G GRANULATED SUGAR
- SALT AND PEPPER, TO SEASON
- 4 TBSP OLIVE OIL
- 50 G UNSALTED BUTTER

Mix the smoked paprika and flour on a plate. On a separate plate, add the crushed garlic to the buttermilk. Cut the tomatoes in half (you'll be serving two halves per portion). Season the tomato slices with salt, pepper and a touch of sugar. Then dip them in the buttermilk mixture. Coat them completely: give them a good drenching. Then remove them and dip them in the flour mixture. If the slice isn't completely covered in the batter, repeat the process.

Heat a frying pan to a medium heat with the olive oil, and once hot, add the butter. When it starts to bubble, add the tomatoes and fry them gently until crispy. This should take about 4 to 6 minutes each side (depending on the size of the tomato).

Serve with good toasted bread and a couple of poached eggs.

CHINESE CHA SIU PORK BUNS

●●●

In reading the title of this recipe, you'd be forgiven for thinking this was a sandwich, but it ain't! These are little balls of pork wrapped in a delicate dough and lightly steamed. This recipe will garner you about 20 of these wee pork gems, so this is perfect if you're entertaining. Served with a delicate salad and dipping sauces, this will be a real treat for your guests as a little starter. What I love about this recipe is that you can get most of the work done the night before, as we marinate the pork overnight.

SERVES 4

- 480 G COOKED PORK (SEE P. 87 FOR MEMPHIS STYLE RIBS, BUT A CUT OF ROASTED BELLY OR FILLET WORKS FINE TOO)
- 1½ TBSP HOISIN SAUCE
- 1½ TBSP LIGHT SOY SAUCE
- 1½ TBSP SWEET SOY SAUCE
- 85 G WHITE SUGAR
- 415 ML WARM WATER (ABOUT 40 DEGREES)
- 1 TBSP ACTIVE DRY YEAST
- 2 KG ALL-PURPOSE FLOUR
- 1 TBSP BAKING POWDER
- 4 TBSP LARD
- 1½ TBSP WHITE SUGAR
- 1½ TBSP DARK SOY SAUCE
- 1½ TBSP OYSTER SAUCE
- 240 ML COLD WATER (FOR THE SAUCE)
- 2 TBSP CORNFLOUR
- 2 TBSP WATER
- 1½ TSP SESAME OIL
- ¼ TSP GROUND WHITE PEPPER

To start, let's sort out the pork. Dice the pork into thick strips, about 2 inches in size. We are going to marinate the meat, and as with most marinades, the longer you leave it the better. Give it at least a couple of hours in the fridge, but you'll get the best results if you leave it overnight. To make the marinade, in a bowl mix the hoisin sauce, the light soy sauce and the sweet soy sauce. Pop the pork in and cover the bowl with cling film.

So, on to the buns. In a bowl, dissolve the 85 g of sugar in 415 ml of warm water, and then add the yeast. Let the mixture stand for ten minutes to let the yeast do its thing, when it'll become frothy. In another bowl, sift the flour and baking powder, stir in the shortening and the yeast mixture, and mix well. When the mixture has formed into a dough, knead it well until it's nice and smooth and elastic. When it is, pop the dough into a greased bowl and cover the bowl with cling film. You want to let the dough rise (in a warm spot in the house) for around 2 hours, until it has almost trebled in size.

In a saucepan, combine the 1½ tablespoons of sugar, 1½ tablespoons of dark soy sauce, the oyster sauce and

240 ml of water, and bring this to a boil. In a glass, combine the cornflour with about 2 tablespoons of water and add this to the saucepan. It will thicken the mixture. Mix in 2 tablespoons of lard, then the sesame oil and the white pepper. Mix well, then let it cool, and then mix in the pork.

Back to the dough, which has now proved. Take the dough out of the bowl and knead it lightly on a floured surface until it's smooth and elastic. Roll the dough out into a long roll and divide it in little parcels (you should get around 20 parcels from this recipe). We're going to place a piece of pork into each parcel, so take a piece of the rolled dough into your hand and pop a piece of the pork into the middle, and wrap the dough around the pork, leaving a little gap at the top: they don't have to be completely covered (like a Scotch egg!). Leave these to stand for about 15 minutes.

Then pop the buns into a steamer and steam for about 12–14 minutes.

To serve, pop them onto a large serving platter and put some dips into small bowls around the plate: light soy sauce, dark soy sauce and any other dips of your choice!

APPETISERS

"A gourmet who thinks of calories is like a tart who looks at her watch."

— JAMES BEARD

"By some people, the meal itself is a long delay between the appetiser and the dessert."

— GERTRUDE BERG

I've never quite figured out where I stand on appetisers. When I go out for dinner, I often find that it's the best part of the entire meal. Often described in the States as 'small plates', they are those dishes that you wish you could have at midnight after a feed of drink, or around late afternoon when you're stuck in a meeting in the office. Let's be honest, if someone came into that meeting at 5.15 p.m. and said 'Anyone fancy a plate of crispy duck salad?' you'd bite their arm off.

These recipes can be taken for what they are. A light lunch. A late breakfast. A cracking starter to a great dinner. Take them however you want. But do take them: they're delicious.

My go-to diner appetiser has always been the Caesar salad, and depending on how hungry I am, I'll add chicken or prawns, or both! Another favourite of mine which I've included here is the split pea and ham hock soup. An absolute winner. A hearty bowl of delicious soup, sprinkled with pieces of tender ham hock. Any fans of the '70s classics will love my take on the prawn cocktail too, another crowd-pleaser.

So whether you're making lunch for yourself, or starting what you hope to be a glorious three-course meal, pick an appetiser here and enjoy!

SPLIT PEA AND HAM HOCK SOUP

⊛⊛⊛⊛⊛⊛⊛⊛⊛⊛⊛⊛⊛⊛⊛⊛⊛⊛⊛⊛⊛⊛⊛⊛⊛⊛⊛⊛⊛⊛⊛⊛⊛⊛⊛⊛⊛

This is my type of cooking: a one-pot wonder, almost. It's a winter warmer, full of flavour, and it's easy to make, and easy on your pocket too. Ham hocks are what I use for this recipe; they are so easy to get from your butcher, and not expensive. This recipe sits well as a family dinner and equally well as a dinner-party main course. Delish.

SERVES 4

- 4 HAM HOCKS
- 1 TBSP OLIVE OIL
- 1-INCH CHUNK OF GINGER, PEELED
- 1½ MEDIUM ONIONS, 1 DICED AND THE REMAINING ½ AS LARGE CHUNKS
- 5 CARROTS, 1 WHOLE AND PEELED, REMAINDER DICED
- 3 CELERY STALKS, DICED
- 1 TBSP DRIED THYME
- SALT AND PEPPER TO SEASON
- 500 ML CHICKEN STOCK
- 500 G SPLIT PEAS
- 2 TBSP BUTTER
- 2 SLICES WHITE BREAD
- 1 TBSP FRESH LEMON JUICE
- 165 G CRÈME FRAÎCHE

Let's start this one off by sorting out the ham hocks. Simply pop them into a large pot of water (enough to cover the meat) with half an onion (chunks), 1 peeled carrot and a 1-inch piece of peeled ginger, bring to the boil, and then simmer and cook for 2 hours. The meat will fall off the bone when cooked. When the ham hocks are ready, remove from the pot and set aside to cool. Don't discard the bones though, as we'll use them to flavour our soup.

For the soup, in a large pan, heat the oil and the butter, then add the onion (diced), carrots, celery and thyme, and season with salt and pepper. Cook for about 8 minutes, until the veg start to soften. Then add the chicken stock, the ham bones, the split peas. Bring to a boil, then reduce to a simmer and cook until the peas are soft: this will take around 30−45 minutes.

Make your croutons while this is cooking. Simply dice the bread into bite-size cubes, put them onto a baking tray, and sprinkle with some salt and a drizzle of oil. Pop them into the bottom of the oven at 160 degrees, and bake until the croutons are golden (it should take about 5−7 minutes).

When the soup is cooked, remove the ham bones. Take half of the liquid out, blitz it in your food processor and then return it to the rest of the soup in the pot.

With your ham now cool, shred the ham with a couple of forks and put it into the soup, but hold a little back to dress the bowl when serving. Add salt and pepper to taste, and a little lemon juice. To serve, pour the soup into bowls and garnish with the shredded ham and croutons. Drizzle a little crème fraiche around the ham.

Enjoy!

"Probably one of the most private things in the world is an egg before it is broken."

— M.F.K. FISHER

"Training is everything. The peach was once a bitter almond; cauliflower is nothing but cabbage with a college education."

— MARK TWAIN

MATZO BALL SOUP

WITH PULLED CHICKEN

● ●

According to the International Federation of Competitive Eating (yes, this does exist, trust me), the world's largest matzo ball was prepared by Chef Jon Wirtis of Sclomo and Vito's New York Delicatessen, located in Tucson, Arizona. He created a 193 kg matzo ball for New York's Jewish food festival. And according to majorleagueeating.com, a man by the name of Eric 'Badlands' Booker (I kid you not) holds the world record for eating matzo balls: he devoured twenty-one baseball-sized matzo balls in five minutes and twenty-five seconds.

Now, while I greatly admire these two men and their incredible food feats, this recipe is designed for your kitchen table. It'll serve about six people, and is simplicity itself. I've adapted this Jewish dish, traditionally served at Passover, replacing the matzo meal with breadcrumbs, as the matzo meal can be tricky to get your hands on. It's basically a chicken soup with dumplings. You can also make your own chicken stock but here I'm going for the good old chicken stock cubes. Easy-peasy.

SERVES 6

- 1 TBSP RAPESEED OIL
- 2 LARGE FREE-RANGE EGGS
- 85 ML CLUB SODA
- 680 G BREADCRUMBS
- 1 TBSP FRESH DILL, CHOPPED
- 1 TBSP SALT
- ½ TSP FRESHLY GROUND BLACK PEPPER
- 1 L CHICKEN STOCK
- 3 CHICKEN LEGS, SKINNED AND CUT INTO PIECES
- 2 CARROTS, ROUGHLY CHOPPED
- 1 CELERY STICK, CHOPPED
- 1 MEDIUM WHITE ONION, SLICED
- 2 TBSP FRESH FLAT-LEAF PARSLEY, CHOPPED
- 1 TBSP FRESH CHIVES, CHOPPED

This recipe begins with the matzo balls. In a mixing bowl, add the oil, the eggs and the club soda, and stir well. Then stir in the breadcrumbs, salt and pepper, and then let the mixture chill for about 30 minutes.

After the 30 minutes, get your hands in there and shape the dough into little balls. You can go as big or small as you like (maybe not as big as Mr Booker's attempt), but ideally you want to get about 20 balls from this mixture, so go for between half an inch and an inch per ball.

Into a large pot, over a medium heat, add your chicken stock and the chicken pieces. Bring to the boil, and then simmer for around 30 minutes or until the chicken is cooked. You'll need to skim this stock as the chicken is cooking, just to remove any impurities, as we want the finished soup to be nice and clear, like a broth.

When the chicken is cooked, take it out of the pot and set it aside, letting it cool slightly. Using a couple of forks, pull all of the meat off the chicken, discarding the bones and so on. Then add the little breadcrumb balls to the stock, along with your celery and the carrots, and simmer for another 30 minutes. Then add the sliced onion and cook for another 8 minutes or so until the little balls are cooked through.

To serve, remove from the heat, stir in your shredded chicken, season to taste with salt and pepper, and garnish with the parsley and chives. Depending on whether you go for two or three matzo balls per portion, this can be a light lunch or a filling winter warmer.

CRAB CAKES

WITH BUTTER SAUCE

●●

This is a really simple, tasty dish. The crab cakes themselves are easy to make, and I've chosen to accompany them with a silky butter sauce. You can of course go with a horseradish cream or a simple mayonnaise, but if you're cooking this for a dinner party starter, go with the butter sauce: it brings this elegant dish to another level. Serve with a nice crusty bread and a simple green salad.

SERVES 4

FOR THE CRAB CAKES:
• 1 FREE-RANGE EGG
• 50 G MAYONNAISE
• 1 TBSP DIJON MUSTARD
• 1 TBSP WORCESTERSHIRE SAUCE
• JUICE OF 1½ LEMONS
• A HANDFUL OF FRESH PARSLEY, CHOPPED
• 550 G FRESH WHITE CRABMEAT
• 50 G BREADCRUMBS
• OLIVE OIL

FOR THE BUTTER SAUCE:
• 350 ML WHITE WINE
• 3 SHALLOTS, DICED
• 1 SPRIG OF THYME
• 1 BAY LEAF
• 3 TBSP DOUBLE CREAM
• 300 G BUTTER
• JUICE OF 1 LEMON

Let's kick off by making the crab cakes. In a large bowl, add the egg, the mayonnaise, the mustard, the Worcestershire sauce, the lemon juice and the parsley. Mix well. Gently fold the crabmeat into the mixture, and then add your breadcrumbs. Before we get to shaping them into cakes, let the mixture chill in the fridge for about 30 minutes. If you have used frozen crabmeat (which is fine!) the mixture may seem a little wet, and if it is, just add some more breadcrumbs.

Preheat your oven to 190°C. Take the crab mixture from the fridge and shape into burger-sized patties. Then in a large pan (one that you can pop into the oven later) add a glug of olive oil, and lay the cakes in. You want to brown the cakes on both sides, which should take a couple of minutes per side, then transfer the pan into the oven for about 10 minutes, or until cooked through.

On to the lovely butter sauce. In a small saucepan, add the white wine, the shallots, the thyme and the bay leaf, and reduce this down over a medium heat, until you're left with about 3 or 4 tablespoons of liquid. Then add the cream and bring it back to the boil. When it boils, remove from the heat and add the butter a little at a time, making sure that you keep whisking the mixture continuously. Finish off the sauce by removing the bay and the thyme, then add a squeeze of lemon juice. Don't forget to season the sauce with salt and pepper to taste!

Pop the crab cakes onto a serving plate, add a salad of your choice, and put the sauce on the side in a pot.

FRIED CALAMARI

WITH SWEET CHILLI SAUCE

●◦●

A dish that can be a light lunch, or a dinner party starter, this is a simple and quick recipe that is a real crowd-pleaser. The chilli sauce can be made from scratch, or you can buy a really good jar of your favourite dipping sauce from the supermarket. The key to this recipe is in the frying of the calamari: keep an eye on them, as you don't want to overcook them. As with most things in my life, when it comes to the frying, less is more . . .

SERVES 4

- 480 G CLEANED CALAMARI TUBES
- 500 ML SUNFLOWER OR VEGETABLE OIL (AMOUNT WILL VARY, BUT ENOUGH TO FILL THE PAN BY A COUPLE OF INCHES)
- 180 ML CLUB SODA
- 340 G PLAIN FLOUR
- ½ TSP CAYENNE PEPPER
- PINCH OF SEA SALT
- 4 TBSP CHILLI SAUCE (SEE SIDES, P. 208)
- 6 TBSP HONEY
- ½ TSP SESAME OIL
- A HANDFUL OF SESAME SEEDS

Slice the calamari into bite-size rings, about ¼-inch wide. In a large bowl, pour the club soda in. Pop the calamari rings into the club soda and let them sit happily there for about 10 minutes. In another bowl, add the flour, salt and cayenne pepper and mix together. Set aside.

In a small bowl add the chilli sauce, honey and sesame oil and mix well. Set aside.

Remove the calamari from the club soda and drain well on kitchen paper. Then dredge the calamari, one at a time, into the flour mixture and leave on a plate covered in kitchen paper.

In a wok or deep pan, heat a couple of inches of oil. Get the oil to about 160°C. When ready, drop the calamari in, a couple at a time, and fry for about 1½ minutes to 2 minutes until golden. When done, put them on a sheet of kitchen paper.

Serve in a bowl with the dipping sauce on the side. Sprinkle the dipping sauce with the sesame seeds for an added bit of crunch!

STICKY BAKED BUFFALO WINGS, DUBLIN-STYLE

•••

An absolute staple of diner menus everywhere. Some diners and restaurants have built their reputation on how good their buffalo wings are. Here in Dublin we're spoiled for choice when it comes to spots that serve great wings. Elephant & Castle springs to everyone's minds when asked where to get good wings in Dublin. I've seen their wings almost reduce people to tears. But why is it that chicken wings are called buffalo wings? I know, it keeps me awake at night too. Unsurprisingly, neither the origin nor the name have anything at all to with actual buffalo. I'm reliably informed that the reason they are called so is that they originated in Buffalo, New York, first being served at the Anchor Bar, owned by Frank and Teressa Bellissimo, who bought the place in 1939. In 1964, Teressa had an idea: why not fry chicken wings up and serve them in a hot sauce? Many theories exist about how she came up with the recipe, but the most reliable is the story that her husband Frank revealed in an interview with the New Yorker *in 1980. The bar had received a shipment of wings by accident. They had been expecting other parts of chicken and simply they didn't know what to do with the wings. His wife started experimenting in the kitchen, and hey-ho she came up with the beloved buffalo wings. Thank God for deliveries that go wrong.*

This is my spin on her classic. The 'Dublin-style' element comes from one of our most famous exports: Guinness. You're welcome.

SERVES 4

FOR THE WINGS:
• 1 KG CHICKEN WINGS (ABOUT 14–20 WINGS, DEPENDING ON THEIR SIZE)
• 1 TBSP SESAME OIL
• 1 TBSP SOY SAUCE
• 1 TBSP FRESH LIME JUICE

Let's get started with the wings, and the marinade. Get yourself a large resealable food bag and pop the wings in. Add the sesame oil, soy sauce and lime juice. Seal the bag and mix the wings around, making sure they each get a coating of that beautiful marinade. Pop these in the fridge for around 3 hours so the ingredients can do their thing.

After the 3 hours, preheat your oven to 220°C. Spread the wings on a baking tray and cook for around 20

FOR THE SAUCE:
- 1 TBSP HOISIN SAUCE
- 3 TBSP ORGANIC HONEY
- 1 TBSP SOY SAUCE
- 150 ML GUINNESS
- 2 TSP SESAME OIL
- 1 CLOVE GARLIC, CRUSHED

minutes. While these are in the oven, let's make the sauce for the wings. In a small saucepan, on a medium heat, add the hoisin sauce, honey, soy sauce, Guinness, sesame oil and the garlic. Whisk these together until smooth. Bring to a simmer and cook until the mixture has thickened. It'll take about 5 minutes.

Remove the wings from the oven and brush them with the sauce, making sure to toss them well so they all get a coating. Pop them back in the tray and cook for a further 5 minutes until they are glazed and cooked through.

To serve, pop these bad boys into a big bowl, and if you fancy a dip, I highly recommend a blue cheese one to go along with them (see Sides, p. 206).

CRISPY DUCK SALAD

●●

This is a recipe that I wanted to make sure was in this book. I'm a big fan of duck, but I reckon, probably like most home cooks, I don't cook it enough. My local butcher, Padraig Howley, as with most local butchers, deals in the finest of produce, including duck, and he recommended I try it a few years ago, suggesting a simple roasting recipe. I took his advice, and loved it. So I've been keen to get a duck salad recipe that is easy, tasty, and combines all those beautiful Asian things I love about that type of cuisine. Being able to combine crispy and fresh vegetables sliced wafer-thin, with soft, dark, tender meat, fresh herbs and a sweet and sour dressing, for me, is a thing of joy. I hope you'll share my enthusiasm for this recipe after you've tried it!

SERVES 4

FOR THE SALAD:
- 2 X DUCK BREAST, SKIN ON
- A HANDFUL OF BEAN SPROUTS
- 100 G RICE NOODLES
- A HEAD OF CABBAGE
- 1 CARROT
- 1 RED CHILLI
- 3 SPRING ONIONS
- 2 HANDFULS OF FRESH MINT
- 2 HANDFULS OF FRESH CORIANDER
- 1 TBSP HONEY
- 1 TBSP SOY SAUCE

FOR THE DRESSING:
- JUICE OF 1 LIME
- 2 TBSP FISH SAUCE
- 1 TBSP SUGAR
- 1 RED CHILLI, FINELY CHOPPED

FOR THE GARNISH:
- A HANDFUL OF SALTY PEANUTS
- 4 SHALLOTS
- 2 LIME WEDGES

Let's start with preparing the duck breast. Use a sharp knife to lightly score the skin of the duck breast. Cut away the extra fat on the sides and rub salt into the breast. Place the breast on a cold pan with the skin side downwards and turn on the pan on a medium-high heat. Cook until the fat starts to come away from the duck, frying the breast for 6–8 mins on each side. When the breast is almost done, spread the honey on the crispy skin and pour on the soy sauce, then fry the breast just another minute while the marinade seasons the meat. Set the breast aside to sit for 3–4 minutes before thinly slicing it.

While the duck is frying, start the salad. Pour boiling water onto the rice noodles and let them soak for 5 minutes, before rinsing with cold water. Thinly slice the cabbage, carrot, and spring onions. Chop the herbs and the chilli.

Mix together all ingredients for the dressing.

Combine the noodles, the chopped veg mix and the beansprouts in a large bowl and mix in the dressing. Fry the shallots in a little olive oil, until golden and crispy, then take them off the pan and place onto some kitchen paper to remove the excess oil.

To serve, start with the noodles in a bowl, then lay the duck on top and add the dressing. Finally, squeeze the lime and sprinkle the peanuts and shallots over the dish.

CLASSIC CAESAR SALAD

●●●

This is my favourite salad of all time. I always ordered this in a restaurant, but I never had to guts to make it myself at home. A couple of years ago my nephew Sean was making his confirmation, and I suggested to his mam Karen that I'd do the catering for the day. The first thing I thought of for the menu was this salad. You can find Caesar Salad recipes in thousands of places but this one is a recipe inspired initially by Simon Rimmer, amongst others, and which has become one of my favourites. I've never looked back since. I love making this dish, and taking the time to make the dressing yourself is so worth it: the taste is sensational.

SERVES 4

FOR THE SALAD:
· 2 CHICKEN BREASTS, ON THE BONE, SKIN ON
· SALT AND PEPPER
· 1 TBSP OLIVE OIL
· 150 ML CHICKEN STOCK

FOR THE CROUTONS:
· 200 G WHITE BREAD, DICED
· PINCH OF SALT
· 80 ML OLIVE OIL

FOR THE DRESSING:
· 150 G PARMESAN, GRATED
· 2 TBSP WHITE WINE VINEGAR
· 250 G MAYONNAISE
· 3 TBSP DIJON MUSTARD
· 2 ANCHOVY FILLETS
· PINCH OF SALT
· 50 ML OLIVE OIL
· 1 GARLIC CLOVE, CRUSHED

FOR THE GARNISH:
· 1 COS OR ROMAINE LETTUCE
· 12 ANCHOVIES (TINNED)
· 50 G PARMESAN, SHAVED

Preheat your oven to 200°C.

Let's start with the main event, the chicken. Season the chicken well with salt and pepper. Heat the oil in a frying pan on a medium heat and pop the chicken breasts in, skin-side down. You want to cook this until the skin is crisp and a nice golden colour, which should take about 5 minutes. After 5 minutes, flip the breasts over and cook for a further 2 minutes. When done, take the chicken breasts out of the frying pan and pop them into a roasting dish and add the stock. Try to pour the stock around the meat rather than over it: this will keep the skin nice and crispy. Put the dish into the oven and cook for 20 minutes, or until cooked through. The easiest way to check if it's cooked all the way through is stick a knife into the thickest part of the breast: if the juices run clear, you're good to go. Take the chicken out and set aside to cool slightly.

Now onto the crunch in the salad: the croutons. Simply dice the bread into bite-size cubes, put them onto a baking tray and sprinkle with some salt and a drizzle of oil. Pop them into the bottom of the oven and bake until the croutons are golden, which should take about 5–7 minutes.

Now we turn our attention to the dressing. Put the Parmesan and the white wine vinegar in your food processor and blend until really smooth. Add the mayonnaise, the mustard, the anchovy fillets, salt, olive oil and garlic, and blend again until nice and smooth.

To serve, get yourself a nice salad bowl, pop the lettuce in there and pour some of the dressing on. Gently toss the leaves so each is covered with our creamy dressing. Add the croutons. Dress the salad with the anchovy fillets and add a little more dressing. Carve the chicken breasts and place them across the salad. To finish, shave some Parmesan and drop it over the salad.

CALIFORNIAN COBB SALAD WRAPS

Spending time alone in any diner in California, particularly in LA, you'll hear orders coming in for this dish at a huge rate. I'd heard it so often that one day I ordered it myself. I know, a salad! But this is a salad that is a meal in itself, with chicken, bacon, eggs, lettuce and a dressing that brings everything together, with a lovely Stilton cheese and a little punch of Worcestershire sauce. What I've done with this recipe is put this salad into wraps to make it a party dish suitable for picnics and so on. It could be a lunchbox snack for the kids too.

Where this dish originates has become the subject of much debate. It even ended up in an episode of Curb Your Enthusiasm, one of my favourite shows, where Larry David searches for evidence to prove that another character, Cliff Cobb, has falsely claimed that his grandfather invented the salad. The most plausible story about where this dish came from is that it was the invention of Robert Howard Cobb, the owner of the Hollywood Brown Derby restaurant. Once, he hadn't eaten till almost midnight, so he went into the kitchen and grabbed a few salad leaves, some leftover cooked bacon and some chicken, and tossed it all in a French dressing. Bingo: a salad was born. And what a salad. Thank you, Mr Cobb.

SERVES 4

- 2 FREE-RANGE CHICKEN THIGHS, ON THE BONE, SKIN ON
- SALT AND PEPPER
- 1 LARGE PINCH OF SMOKED PAPRIKA
- OLIVE OIL
- 4 SLICES PANCETTA
- 2 FREE-RANGE EGGS
- 1 HEAD OF LETTUCE, PREFERABLY ROMAINE OR COS
- 1 AVOCADO
- 2 TOMATOES
- A HANDFUL OF SALAD CRESS
- 4 LARGE TORTILLA WRAPS

Preheat your oven to 180°C.

Pop the chicken thighs into a roasting tray. Season with salt and pepper, add the paprika and drizzle with a little olive oil. Make sure the chicken is well coated in the oil and seasoning, and then pop the tray into the oven and cook until a nice golden colour, which should take about 25 minutes. After this time, take the tray out of the oven and place the pancetta across the chicken, and pop the tray back into the oven for a further 10 to 15 minutes, until cooked through. When the chicken has cooked, let it and the pancetta cool slightly.

In a small pot, pop the eggs into some boiling water. If, like me, you like your eggs soft-boiled, this should take

FOR THE SALAD DRESSING:
- 50 G STILTON
- OLIVE OIL
- ½ A BUNCH OF FRESH CHIVES
- 50 ML BUTTERMILK
- 200 G NATURAL YOGHURT
- ½ TSP WORCESTERSHIRE SAUCE
- JUICE OF 1 LEMON

about 6 to 7 minutes. When cooked, take them out, let them cool and then peel the shells off.

Next we'll get the dressing done. Start by crumbling the Stilton into a bowl, and then a good glug of olive oil, followed by the chopped chives. Add the buttermilk, the yoghurt, the Worcestershire sauce and the juice of the lemon, and mix well.

Chop the lettuce, then de-stone the avocado and scoop out the flesh. Pop these onto a serving board. Halve the tomatoes and the eggs. With all of these ingredients now on the serving board, get your knife in there and chop them all up.

Pull the chicken meat off the bone, using a couple of forks, and discard the bones and the skin. Add the chicken meat to your chopped salad on the serving board. Break the pancetta up into crumbs, leaving a few bite-size pieces. Add these to the salad and give everything another chop through.

To serve, drizzle some of the chilled blue cheese dressing over the salad, and garnish with a little cress. Lay your tortilla wraps out and spoon some of the mixture in the middle and fold over. Do the same with all your wraps, and lay them all on a serving dish. Add some of the dressing to a small bowl and serve on the side.

MARDI GRAS PRAWN COCKTAIL

●●

I know, I know, you see the words 'prawn cocktail' and straight away you're transported back to your youth and those visits to the posh auntie's house. She had the best dinner parties, the best the seventies had to offer: fondue, beef Wellington and, of course, that oversized dessert glass stuffed with tepid prawns, limp lettuce and a watery shop-bought Marie Rose sauce. Delish. The trouble with those dinner parties was that that was the menu for the adults, which meant it's what the kids had to eat too – unless you fancied a burnt cocktail sausage.

Well, this is my version of a classic prawn cocktail. This recipe drags that beloved seventies classic into the twenty-first century, using our own mayonnaise and a host of mouth-tingling spices like cayenne pepper and paprika. Using those southern influences again, and to give you a sense of Mardi Gras, this lifts this dish into a different world. A world you'll be happy to dine in . . .

SERVES 4

- 400 G COOKED PRAWNS (FROZEN ONES ARE PERFECTLY FINE TO USE HERE)
- 200 ML LIGHT BEER
- 100 G PLAIN FLOUR
- ½ TSP PAPRIKA
- ¼ TSP CAYENNE PEPPER
- ½ TSP GARLIC POWDER
- 200 G ICEBERG LETTUCE, CHOPPED
- 150 G MAYONNAISE (SEE P. 205)
- 75 G HOISIN SAUCE
- 50 G FRESH DILL, CHOPPED
- JUICE OF 1 LEMON
- 4 LEAVES ICEBERG LETTUCE, LEFT WHOLE
- 50 G RADISH
- ½ CUCUMBER
- SEA SALT, TO SEASON

First things first: prep the prawns. Make sure they are all clean, with the veins removed. Then drop them into the beer and let them soak up all that lovely beery goodness for about ten minutes. Mix the flour, paprika, cayenne and garlic powder on a plate. Turn your deep fat fryer to 160°C. Alternatively, heat 500mls of vegetable oil in a saucepan, over a medium heat. While you're waiting for this to heat, make the cocktail sauce. Mix the mayonnaise, hoisin sauce, dill and lemon juice together into a jar or a bowl. Mix well. And that's the sauce done.

So, let's prep the lettuce. Get one of the whole leaves of iceberg, as you're going to use it like a tortilla wrap. Place it on a plate. Slice the radishes, nice and thin, and, using a vegetable peeler, shave the cucumber into nice thin strips. Divide the chopped lettuce between the four lettuce wraps, and do the same with the sliced radish and cucumber.

Remove the prawns from the beer and add them to the flour mix. Coat well and immediately deep fry until beautifully golden brown, which normally takes 2–3 minutes, depending on the size of your prawns. When cooked, drain off the excess oil and place them on kitchen paper. Season with sea salt. Divide them equally between your lettuce wraps. Spoon some of your dressing mix on top of the prawns, and devour . . .

For the purposes of this book, I've photographed my version of how I wished my auntie's prawn cocktail had looked. Complete with dessert glass.

ROAST EAR OF CORN
WITH CORIANDER CHOPHOUSE-STYLE BUTTER

● ●

'The Chophouse'. Along with 'the Steakhouse', it's one of the best things to see above the door of a restaurant you're about to eat in. One of my favourite dining experiences in the US happened during a filming trip in Dallas. I was there filming Chain Reactions, *a documentary series for RTE1. On our third or fourth night there, our director, my good pal Gerry Hoban (a man who has an amazing knowledge of worldwide cuisines, and who is a fine cook himself) suggested that we treat ourselves and go to an upmarket chophouse. We found ourselves in fine surroundings in one of the best chop- and steakhouses Dallas had to offer. The name escapes me, but that meal has never left me. I ordered pork chops and American mash. When my plate arrived, I was amazed to see two 6 oz. pork chops standing on their sides, divided by a mound of hot, creamy, silky American mash. Gerry took one look at the plate and said, 'You'll never finish that.' I'd only know Gerry a few months. Needless to say, all that was left on the plate were two bones. My lasting memory was the taste of that chophouse butter. Try it. It'll make an impression on you too.*

SERVES 4

- 4 EARS OF CORN WITH LEAVES ON
- 250 G UNSALTED BUTTER, SOFTENED
- 1 SHALLOT, FINELY CHOPPED
- 2 GARLIC CLOVES, CRUSHED
- 50 ML WORCESTERSHIRE SAUCE
- 100 G SUNDRIED TOMATO
- 40 G FRESH CORIANDER, CHOPPED
- 40 G ROSEMARY, CHOPPED
- 40 G THYME, CHOPPED
- 40 G PARSLEY, CHOPPED
- SALT AND PEPPER

Preheat your oven to 160°C.

Place the 4 ears of corn straight on to the middle shelf and roast for about 30 minutes.

While they're cooking, let's crack on with the coriander chophouse-style butter. Take 50g of the butter and melt in a small pan on a medium heat. When it starts to bubble, add the chopped shallot and cook gently until soft, without colouring: this should take about 8 minutes. Add the crushed garlic and cook for another 2 minutes. Add the Worcestershire sauce and reduce this down, which will take a couple of minutes. Remove the pan from the heat and allow the shallot mix to cool.

While the mix cools, blend the remaining butter in a food processor until the butter turns white. Add the sundried tomato and chopped herbs and blend. Then add the shallot mix and season with salt and pepper. Scrape the butter mix into a bowl and leave aside until needed.

When the corn is cooked, carefully remove from the oven and very carefully peel back the leaves. These will be very hot! Spread the butter over the corn and season with salt and pepper. Serve to the table immediately.

MAINS

"Love and sausages are alike. Can never have enough of them."

— TRIXIE KOONTZ

"A fruit is a vegetable with looks and money. Plus, if you let fruit rot, it turns into wine, something Brussels sprouts never do."

— P.J. O'ROURKE

Nigel Mearns with Simon

When it comes to the main event, the main course, this was the chapter of the book that gave me the most sleepless nights. What dishes to leave out? There are so many great dishes that I've eaten in diners across the States that haven't made it in. When I'm at home, food channels are all that I watch on TV. (That and the odd Manchester United match.) I spent so many hours watching programmes about diners (you know the ones I'm talking about!) with a paper and pen in my hand, scribbling frantically as I whispered, 'Oh yeah, that's got to be in there' or 'God, I'd love to be able to make that at home' etc. etc. It got to the point where I had about 130 dishes written down. So the choice had to be narrowed down, if for no other reason than to keep my editor's blood pressure on an even keel! These are the ones that have made it, these glorious dozen dishes that would grace any diner table. There's plenty of choice in there, from meat to fish to pasta. I've even gone over the border from the US and featured a Canadian diner classic. When I saw this dish being made on one of my favourite shows, *You Gotta Eat Here!*, hosted by the brilliant John Catucci, I had one of those moments where I sat up and said out loud, 'That's definitely going in the book.' The poutine. What a dish. If you don't know where to start in this chapter, start with the poutine. You'll be hooked . . .

CHICKEN POT PIE

●●

In an attempt to educate as well as provide you with some cracking recipes, my research on this dish threw up this fact: the 'pot pie' originated in Greece. Yes, Greece. I had no idea either. The Greeks cooked meats and placed them in open pastry shells that were called Artocreas. And it was the Romans (what have they ever done for us??) who added the top crust making chicken pot pie into an actual pie.

When it comes to the pastry on this pie, I always use the shop-bought puff pastry. If you have the time and the inclination to make the fresh stuff, go for it, I'll admire you from afar. I just never have the time, nor the patience. Most chefs will tell you that the shop-bought is as good, so that's good enough for me. My little twist on the traditional recipe is to add crispy bacon to the pie. This gives the dish another layer of flavour. Let's go!

SERVES 4-6

- 1 TBSP OLIVE OIL
- 2 TBSP BUTTER
- 900 G BONELESS SKINLESS CHICKEN THIGHS, CUT INTO PIECES
- 2 MEDIUM LEEKS, WASHED AND CHOPPED INTO ½-INCH PIECES
- 2 CARROTS, ROUGHLY CHOPPED
- 3 STICKS CELERY, FINELY SLICED
- 2 TSP DRIED THYME
- 2½ TBSP FLOUR
- 1 GLASS WHITE WINE
- 1 GLASS WATER
- 400 ML WHOLE MILK
- SALT AND PEPPER
- 180 G BACON
- 450 G PUFF PASTRY
- 1 EGG, BEATEN

Like most of my one-pot wonders, this starts off by building a base of flavour. In a large casserole pot over a medium heat, add a little olive oil and butter, and when warm, add the chicken, leeks, carrots, celery and the thyme. Cook this for around 15 minutes, then add the flour and continue to stir for a couple of minutes.

Add the glass of wine, followed by a glass of water, and then the milk. Cover the dish with a tight-fitting lid and simmer on the stove for 20 to 30 minutes, until the chicken is tender. Keep an eye on it and stir it every so often so it doesn't stick to the bottom of the pot. The sauce should be loose, but quite thick. If the sauce is a little too loose, continue to cook it with the lid off until it thickens slightly, and if you need to you can add a little more flour. (If you are adding flour, make sure to stir it in so it doesn't go clumpy!) Season the dish with a little salt and freshly ground black pepper.

While this is cooking away, take your rashers and cut them into 2-inch pieces, pop them into a frying pan with a little olive oil, and fry them until nice and crisp.

Preheat your oven to 220°C.

And so, to assemble the pie. Pour the chicken stew into a large pie dish. Spread the cooked rashers evenly around the top of the stew.

Roll out your pastry, not too thin, to about ¼-inch thick. Egg-wash the rim of the pie dish and drape over the pastry, using a knife to trim the edge of the dish. Egg-wash the top of the pastry to make it go golden while cooking. If you can, crimp the edges of the pastry around the edges. You can use the back of your knife to make a nice criss-cross pattern across the top of the pie. This will also allow the pastry to go crisp and flaky. Pop the pie into the centre of your oven and cook for about 30–40 minutes, until golden on top.

PULLED PORK MAC AND CHEESE

●●●

There aren't many dishes that can claim their own day on the calendar. However, if you happen to be in the United States on any given July 14th, you'll be there on 'National Macaroni and Cheese Day'. I know, I'm also checking flights on the Internet now as we speak. So, what can you add to an American classic to make it even better? How about another American classic? Pulled pork. Ah yes, two words that when I see them on a menu, I'm ordering the dish. This recipe is a great family dinner, a real crowd-pleaser. Cook this in a big casserole dish, put it in the middle of the table, and let them at it . . .

SERVES 6

- 1 TBSP VEGETABLE OIL
- 450 G MACARONI
- 180 G BUTTER
- 250 G PLAIN FLOUR
- 950 ML MILK
- 400 G GRUYÈRE, GRATED
- 200 G CHEDDAR, GRATED
- ½ TSP GROUND NUTMEG
- 400 G PULLED PORK (SEE P. 211)
- 125 G BREADCRUMBS
- SALT AND PEPPER TO SEASON

Preheat your oven to 190°C.

Into a large pot of boiling water, add a little vegetable oil (to stop the pasta sticking together), then add the macaroni and cook according to the directions on the package (normally it's around 6–8 minutes). When cooked, drain well and set aside.

In a pot, melt 150 g of butter and add the flour. Cook this mixture over a low heat for about 2 minutes, stirring the mixture with a whisk. As you're whisking, add the milk and whisk for another couple of minutes until the consistency is thick and smooth. Take this pot off the heat and add both the Gruyère and Cheddar cheeses, nutmeg, and add salt and pepper to season. Pour in the cooked macaroni and the pulled pork, and stir the mixture well. Then layer the mixture into a casserole dish. To top the dish off, melt the remaining 30 g of butter and add in the breadcrumbs, and sprinkle them on top of the macaroni.

Pop the casserole dish into the oven and cook for about 30–35 minutes until the sauce is bubbling and the breadcrumbs on the top are nice and brown. To serve, add a little sprinkle of cheese.

CLASSIC MEAT LOAF

WITH THE BEST MASH IN IRELAND

●●

In 2007, meat loaf was voted the seventh-favourite dish in the United States, according to Good Housekeeping. In another poll on nbc.com in 2016, it didn't even make the top ten. But fear not, my friends, if 2016 and Brexit and Donald Trump taught us anything, it's not to listen to poll results! Meat loaf, in my humble opinion, has to be in the top five diner dishes of all time. This slice of home can hold its head high amongst all those other diner classics as a timeless crowd-pleaser. There are as many meat loaf recipes as there are political analysts, and it's really up to you which one you go for. Traditionally a meat loaf in the States would be eaten with some kind of sauce or relish, or with a simple brown gravy. I'm serving mine alongside creamy mashed potatoes with roasted garlic, the ones that Daniel Clifford from MasterChef described as 'the best mash potatoes in Ireland'. See if he's right! Try it, and you'll have them smiling from ear to ear.

SERVES 4-6

FOR THE MEAT LOAF:
- 25 G UNSALTED BUTTER
- 1 MEDIUM WHITE ONION, FINELY CHOPPED
- 2 CELERY STALKS, FINELY CHOPPED
- 1/2 GREEN PEPPER, FINELY CHOPPED
- 4 SPRING ONIONS, FINELY CHOPPED
- 2 GARLIC CLOVES, CRUSHED
- 1 TBSP FRESH PARSLEY, FINELY CHOPPED
- 2 TBSP CHILLI SAUCE
- 1 TBSP WORCESTERSHIRE SAUCE
- 2 BAY LEAVES
- 85 G EVAPORATED MILK
- 170 G TOMATO KETCHUP
- 700 G MINCED RIB OF BEEF
- 170 G MINCED PORK OR SAUSAGE MEAT
- 2 FREE-RANGE EGGS
- 2 OR 3 LARGE HANDFULS OF BREADCRUMBS

Preheat your oven to 180°C.

Let's get the roasted garlic for the mash sorted first. Pop your whole garlic bulb into some tinfoil, coat in in some olive oil, wrap it tight and pop it into a low oven, about 180°C, for about 35 minutes.

To start the meat loaf, melt the butter in a large saucepan, and add the onion, celery, green pepper, spring onions, garlic, parsley, chilli sauce, Worcestershire sauce and the bay leaves. Cook over a gentle heat, stirring occasionally, for about 6 minutes.

Add the evaporated milk and the ketchup and continue to cook for a further 2 minutes. After the 2 minutes, remove from the heat and allow the mixture to cool. Discard the bay leaves.

Place the beef and the pork in a large bowl, then add the eggs, breadcrumbs and the vegetable mixture from the other saucepan, and season to taste. If you feel

FOR THE AMERICAN MASH:

- 5 LARGE ROOSTER POTATOES
- 75 G BUTTER
- 100 ML CREAM
- 50 G PARMESAN
- A HANDFUL OF CHIVES, FINELY CHOPPED
- 1 GARLIC BULB
- SALT AND PEPPER, TO SEASON

the mixture is too wet, add some more breadcrumbs. Sprinkle the parmesan into the meat loaf mixture, then pop the mixture in an ungreased roasting dish. Drizzle a little olive oil onto a piece of tinfoil and place this on top of the meat loaf (oil side down, to stop it burning) and bake for 25 minutes. Then turn your oven up to 200°C and bake for a further 35–40 minutes. After 30 minutes, remove the tinfoil so you can get a nice crust on the meat loaf.

While the meat loaf is cooking, time to get the potatoes sorted. Peel and quarter the potatoes, then pop into a pot of water and cook on a medium heat until soft. In a small saucepan, heat the butter and the cream – don't boil the mixture, just heat it through. Take your roasted garlic (which has now cooled down slightly), remove the skin and crush with the back of a knife into a paste (making 1 tablespoon of crushed roasted garlic).

When the potatoes are cooked, drain them and pass them through a potato ricer, then add a little of the cream and butter mixture and whip with a spatula. If the mixture is a little dry, add some more of the cream and butter mixture. Add in the crushed roasted garlic and mix again.

To serve, slice the meat loaf, pop onto a plate, and add a helping of the mash alongside. To garnish the mash, sprinkle some of the chopped chives across the top.

"Cooking is like love. It should be entered into with abandon or not at all."

— HARRIET VAN HORNE

"Never order barbecue in a place that also serves quiche."

— LEWIS GRIZZARD

"LOVE ME TENDER" MEMPHIS RIBS

● ●

Who doesn't like a rack of ribs? That tender, sweet pork smothered in a tangy barbeque sauce that seems to get better with every bite. Delicious. This a dish that can put a diner on the map. There are of course joints in the US that just do ribs, and nothing else. One place that springs to mind features in my favourite TV show of the past few years, House of Cards. *Freddy's Ribs is the sanctuary that Frank Underwood (played by Kevin Spacey) sneaks into, day or night, to seek some peace and a (paper) plate of Freddy's world-famous ribs. I've always rated Spacey as one of the finest actors of our generation, but I reckon the ribs the props department provided on the shoot days must have been the real deal, as the joy that rolls across Spacey's face as he tucks in can't be faked, even by one of the greatest. My recipe has an Irish twist, using stout to cook the ribs in.*

SERVES 4

- 50 G MUSCOVADO SUGAR
- 1 TBSP SMOKED PAPRIKA
- 1 TBSP GROUND CUMIN
- ½ TBSP GARLIC POWDER
- ½ TBSP CHILLI FLAKES
- 4 FULL RACKS OF BABY BACK RIBS
- 200 ML GUINNESS
- 500 ML PASSATA
- 1 TBSP TREACLE

To start, let's make the rub for the ribs. In a large bowl, add the sugar, the paprika, the cumin, the garlic powder and the chilli flakes. Pop the ribs in there and rub the mix all around them, making sure the ribs are fully coated. Ideally, try and let the ribs sit in the rub for a couple of hours before cooking, to let all of the spices work their way into the meat.

Preheat your oven to 150°C.

Place the ribs on a raised rack and place the rack into a deep baking tray. Pour the Guinness into the tray underneath the ribs and cover the whole thing with tinfoil. Pop this into the oven and cook for 2 hours. This is low and slow cooking at its finest!

After two hours, remove from the oven, take the ribs out and set aside. Pour the cooking juices into a pan and cook over a medium heat to reduce this down by half. Add the passata and the treacle and reduce again until you end up with a nice thick mixture that we can use to glaze our ribs.

Using a pastry brush, glaze the ribs with the sticky reduction and pop them under a high heat on the grill, so we can get a good char on them. This will only take a few minutes. Repeat the process again with glaze.

To serve, stack the racks of ribs onto a large serving dish and drizzle over the rest of the glaze. Finger-licking good, as they say . . .

CAJUN SHRIMP LINGUINI

WITH ARRABIATA-STYLE SAUCE

● ●

Italian food is without question my favourite type of cuisine. And when it comes to diners, I love the Italian offerings that are on the menus, from chicken Parm sandwiches, to spaghetti and meatballs, to the luscious desserts like tiramisu; it's often the direction I'll go when it comes to ordering my lunch. This recipe is a great lunch dish, and it's easy to make. Using dried pasta is more than acceptable: there's such good quality on offer these days that it's a no-brainer when making dishes like this. I, like a lot of people, don't eat enough fish, but with a dish like this it's easy to put it on the weekly rota at home. This sauce, sugo all'arrabbiata, as the Italians call it, lifts this dish to the next level. The word arrabbiata means 'angry' in Italian, referring to the use of chillies in the sauce. If, like me, you're a wuss when it comes to chillies and heat, stick with one chilli, as quoted in the recipe. If not, and you're a daredevil, pop another in it. The choice, as they say on Blind Date, *is yours . . .*

SERVES 4

- 400 G DRIED LINGUINI
- 3 TBSP GOOD OLIVE OIL
- 1 CHILLI, DESEEDED AND FINELY CHOPPED
- 2 GARLIC CLOVES, FINELY SLICED
- 1½ TSP CAJUN SPICE
- 350 G LARGE PRAWNS, DEVEINED
- 2 PLUM TOMATOES, DESEEDED AND FINELY CHOPPED
- JUICE AND ZEST OF 1 LEMON
- 1 BUNCH OF FLAT-LEAF PARSLEY, CHOPPED

Get a large pot of boiling water on the go and add a good pinch of sea salt. Lots of people don't season their water when making pasta, but according to the best in the business it's essential, as you're getting flavour into the pasta right from the off. Cook the pasta as per instructions on the package and, when cooked, drain and keep warm. Keep a couple of spoonfuls of the pasta-cooking liquor back, as we'll add these to the sauce.

Speaking of the sauce, let's do it. In a pan over a medium heat, add the olive oil, the chilli, the garlic and the Cajun spice. Allow these to cook for a couple of minutes to flavour the oil. Then add the prawns and cook them for about one minute, keeping the pan moving all the time so the prawns get coated in that flavour-packed oil. Add the tomato and the zest and juice of a lemon and then remove from the heat. Add the cooked linguini to the pan and toss through the sauce, along with three tablespoons of the reserved pasta-cooking liquor. Check the seasoning and add salt and pepper if needed.

To serve, pop the pasta and prawns into a large bowl, drizzle with the sauce, and garnish with a sprinkle of the chopped parsley.

CHUCK BEEF BURGER

WITH MONTEREY JACK CHEESE AND HOT PASTRAMI

• •

When you mention the word 'diner', the word 'burger' normally pops into your head soon after. A good burger is truly one of the great dishes of the world. There are a few things that I wanted to feature in my burger, some of my favourite things. One is fried onions, a must for me on a burger: they add a lovely sweetness to the dish. The buns: brioche, of course. One of the things I love about eating a burger in a diner in the States is that when you pick it up, the bread almost collapses around the burger. The burger is the star, not the bread. But if you go with brioche buns, it'll be worth it. Then the hot pastrami: my favourite deli sandwich filler, and amazing on a burger. Then, the small matter of the cheese. I've gone for a Monterey Jack cheese, a creamy melting cheese that's a perfect companion for hot beef. And speaking of the beef, I've carried out a ridiculous amount of research into the perfect burger beef. What you're looking for is an 80/20 mix of beef to fat. I've gone for chuck beef: a great cut of the meat and gorgeous in a burger. Your friendly neighbourhood butcher will provide you with the perfect burger meat; just ask. Finally, there's the burger sauce, a little zing to spread on the buns to accompany that meat and cheese, and this sauce recipe cuts through it beautifully. Hungry yet? Let's cook . . .

SERVES 4

FOR THE BURGERS:
• 2 TBSP WORCESTERSHIRE SAUCE
• 1 TSP CHINESE FIVE-SPICE
• 960 G MINCED CHUCK BEEF, WITH 20% FAT
(YOUR BUTCHER WILL SORT THIS FOR YOU)
• SALT AND PEPPER, TO SEASON

FOR THE BURGER SAUCE:
• 1 TSP SMOKED PAPRIKA
• 100 ML HOISIN SAUCE
• 2 TBSP MAYONNAISE
• 2 SMALL GHERKINS, CHOPPED
• JUICE OF HALF A LEMON

Preheat the oven to 175°C. We'll kick off by making the burger mix. In a bowl add the Worcestershire sauce, the Chinese five-spice mix and the minced beef, and season well with salt and pepper. Don't be shy with the salt: these burgers can take it! When you have the spices mixed well into the beef, divide the mixture into four 240 g balls. Wet your hands with cold water, and then take the meatballs and shape them into burger patties about 1 inch thick. When you have all four done, pop them onto a lined baking tray, cover them and let them sit in the fridge for about 30 minutes to firm up.

While these are in the fridge, we'll make the burger sauce. In a small bowl, simply mix together the smoked paprika, hoisin sauce, mayonnaise, chopped gherkins and lemon juice.

CHUCK BEEF BURGER

TO SERVE:
- 8 SLICES MONTEREY JACK CHEESE
- 16 THIN SLICES PASTRAMI
- A COUPLE OF KNOBS OF BUTTER, MELTED
- 1 MEDIUM RED ONION, FINELY SLICED
- 4 BRIOCHE BURGER BUNS
- 2 BEEF TOMATOES, SLICED
- 1 SMALL HEAD OF BABY GEM LETTUCE, WASHED
- OLIVE OIL

Now to cook the burgers. If you have a griddle pan, put it over a medium heat. The griddle pan is great to get those beautiful marks on the burger, but if you haven't got a griddle, a standard ovenproof pan will do. Take the burgers out of the fridge and let them come to room temperature before you cook them. Add a little olive oil to your pan, get it nice and hot, and pop the burgers in. We're looking to get a nice char on the outside of the burger, so cook them for about 2 minutes on each side. Place the pan into the oven and cook for about 6 minutes or until done. I like my burgers medium, but go with what you prefer.

When ready, take the burgers out of the oven, but leave them in the pan. Place a slice of cheese and a couple of slices of the pastrami over each of the burgers and pop them back into the oven, and turn the oven off! This will heat the pastrami and melt the cheese (a sentence I'll never tire of saying).

In another small pan, add a drizzle of olive oil and a knob of butter and sweat down your onions until coloured and soft. When done, drain on kitchen paper.

To serve, spread a little melted butter on the brioche burger buns and heat them in your pan for a minute. Next, spread some of your burger sauce on both halves of the bun, and then layer on some lettuce, a couple of slices of tomato and the fried onions. Add the burger, cheese and pastrami, then skewer the bun top on with a burger skewer (yes, there is such a thing), and enjoy!

LOUISIANA-STYLE CHICKEN THIGHS

WITH SMOKED PAPRIKA MAYONNAISE

● ●

Louisiana was of course founded by the French, leading to the development of a style of cooking known as Louisiana Creole, which, being based on a French aesthetic, has an emphasis on complex sauces and slow cooking. Here endeth the history lesson. This recipe is neither complex nor slow. The slowest part of the recipe is waiting overnight as the magic spice-mix marinade does its thing with the chicken thighs in the fridge. I've paired the chicken with a beautiful smoky mayo, and yes, we are going to make our own mayonnaise from scratch! This is a great recipe that can be wheeled out in the summer as a barbeque staple, or on those cold winter nights, be served with rich, creamy American-style mashed potatoes (see p. 82). A dish for all seasons and occasions!

SERVES 4

FOR THE SPICE MIX:
- ½ TSP GARLIC SALT
- ½ TSP JAMAICAN JERK SPICE
- ½ TSP TURMERIC

FOR THE CHICKEN:
- 12 SMALL BONELESS, SKINLESS CHICKEN THIGHS
- 100 G PLAIN FLOUR
- 300 ML BUTTERMILK
- 400 G BREADCRUMBS
- 40 G THYME, CHOPPED
- SALT AND PEPPER
- OLIVE OIL, FOR FRYING
- 40 G FRESH PARSLEY, CHOPPED

This recipe starts the night before you want to serve the dish. The night before, take the spices from the spice mix, put them into a large food bag, add the chicken thighs, coat thoroughly, and leave them in the fridge to work their magic overnight.

The next day, preheat your oven to 160°C. Remove the chicken from the fridge and allow come to room temperature.

Get yourself organised with three large bowls. Put the flour in one, the buttermilk in the second, and the breadcrumbs mixed with the chopped thyme in the third bowl. Season all three with salt and pepper.

Taking the chicken thighs one at a time, dredge them in the flour, then the milk, and finally the breadcrumbs. When finished, place them on a layer of greaseproof paper.

FOR THE SMOKED PAPRIKA MAYONNAISE:
- 15 ML DIJON MUSTARD
- 2 EGG YOLKS
- 15 ML LEMON JUICE
- 200 ML VEGETABLE OIL
- 2 ML SMOKED PAPRIKA

Heat a frying pan or large skillet on a medium-high heat. Add a nice drop of oil, and when hot, start cooking the chicken, colouring gently on each side; it should take about two minutes each side. You don't want too much colour, as you'll be finishing them off in the oven. Place the chicken thighs on a good-sized ovenproof dish with some greaseproof paper on the bottom and cook in the oven for about 20 minutes.

To make the mayonnaise, in a bowl whisk the egg yolk with the Dijon mustard and lemon juice. Add in the vegetable oil in a drizzle, while whisking constantly until you get a stiff mayonnaise consistency. Season with salt and pepper and add in the smoked paprika. Put in a small bowl and serve on the side of the chicken thighs.

You can serve them with a large chopped salad to feed the masses, or some home fries for a family dinner — whatever takes your fancy!

TAGLIATELLE AND MEATBALL RAGU

This dish is on the menu in our house at least once a week. It's probably the dish I most enjoy cooking. I'm a huge fan of Italian food and I love the smells in the kitchen as this pot of deliciousness cooks away for hours. This recipe has built over the years. I normally buy my meatballs from a good butcher, but one day attempted to make my own. There is a vast number of meatball recipes out there, but this one happens to be my favourite. Another thing that I love about this recipe is the quantity, and I don't just mean it's a large serving; it's the fact that you can make up this batch of meatballs and freeze them. Also, when cooked you can use the meatballs in a bread roll and make your very own meatball subs!

SERVES 4

• 500 G DRIED TAGLIATELLE

FOR THE MEATBALLS:
• 125 G BREADCRUMBS
• 3 GARLIC CLOVES, CRUSHED
• 1 MEDIUM ONION, FINELY DICED
• 1 TBSP SALT
• 1 TBSP DRIED PARSLEY
• 1 TBSP DRIED BASIL
• ½ TSP DRIED OREGANO
• PINCH OF BLACK PEPPER
• PINCH OF DRIED SAGE
• 450 G GROUND BEEF
• 450 G GROUND PORK
• 2 FREE-RANGE EGGS

We'll start with the meatballs. When you're cooking with meat, it's important to start with the meat at room temperature, so take the meat out of the fridge about 30 minutes before you start.

Preheat your oven to 200°C and prep a roasting tray by lining it with tinfoil and rubbing a little olive oil on it.

In a large mixing bowl, combine the breadcrumbs, crushed garlic, diced onion, salt, parsley, basil, oregano, pepper and the sage. Mix together. Add the ground beef and pork, and the eggs, then gently mix these through. Using your hands (get stuck in there!), scoop out the meat mixture and roll into meatballs. You're looking for a size smaller than a golf ball, and you should get around 25 meatballs from this quantity.

Place the meatballs on to your roasting tray. Pour a cup of hot water around the meatballs, and cover them loosely with another sheet of tinfoil. Pop them into the oven and cook for around 25 minutes.

While this is cooking, let's get the sauce started. Into a large pot, drop in a little olive oil, and when warm

TAGLIATELLE AND MEATBALL RAGU

FOR THE RAGU:
- OLIVE OIL
- 1 LEEK, WASHED AND FINELY CHOPPED
- 1 MEDIUM ONION, FINELY SLICED
- 1 ORANGE PEPPER, FINELY SLICED
- 1 RED PEPPER, FINELY SLICED
- 2 GARLIC CLOVES, CRUSHED
- 1 X 400 G TIN OF CHOPPED TOMATOES
- 500 ML CHICKEN STOCK
- 50 G PARMESAN, GRATED

add in the leek, onion, peppers and the garlic. Sweat these down for about 10 minutes; you just want the veg to soften slightly. Add in the tin of tomatoes and stir through. Then add your chicken stock.

When the meatballs have had 25 minutes in the oven, remove them and pop them into the sauce. On a low heat, let these bubble away for a good 90 minutes. A couple of minutes before you serve, add a little of the grated Parmesan into the sauce.

Pop the pasta into a pot of boiling water, add a little salt and a drop of olive oil, and cook as per instructions on the package. When ready, drain the pasta, keep a couple of tablespoons of the cooking liquor and add these to the ragu. Drop the pasta into the meatballs and ragu pot, and stir through gently.

Serve in large bowls, sprinkle with a little grated Parmesan, and treat yourself to some good garlic bread alongside.

GUINNESS-BRAISED BEEF POUTINE

●●

The poutine. Nope, I'd never heard of it either – until I started watching what is now one of my favourite shows, You Gotta Eat Here!, *presented by the brilliant Canadian comedian John Catucci. In his show, he travels around Canada and the US visiting some of the best delis and diners, finding out why the locals love them so much. He even visited Dublin for an episode and loved what he ate here! As he says himself, John is no chef, but he loves to eat, and boy does he eat on this show! A dish that kept popping up on menus was the Poutine, a Canadian diner classic that has French influences and is universally adored. When I first saw John tuck into this dish of fries, braised beef, cheese curds and gravy, I was sold. And I think you will be too. I've tailored a recipe to give this an Irish twist, which involves Guinness. It takes a little time and effort, this one, but boy it's worth the effort, and if you have any of the beef left over, it can be used as a sandwich filling or as a great pizza topping.*

SERVES 4-6

- 1.5 KG BEEF SHORT RIBS, ON THE BONE
- 3 TBSP OLIVE OIL
- 1 MEDIUM WHITE ONION
- PINCH OF SALT AND PEPPER
- 4 GARLIC CLOVES, CRUSHED
- 4 TBSP TOMATO PUREE
- 330 ML GUINNESS
- 500 ML OF CHICKEN STOCK
- 1 SPRIG OF FRESH ROSEMARY
- 2 SPRIGS OF FRESH THYME
- 6 ROOSTER POTATOES
- 50 G UNSALTED BUTTER
- 2 TBSP PLAIN FLOUR
- 240 G CHEESE CURDS OR GRATED IRISH CHEDDAR
- A HANDFUL OF FRESH PARSLEY, CHOPPED

Preheat your oven to 180°C.

Let's start by prepping the beef ribs for the oven, so in a bowl add around 250g of plain flour and season with salt and pepper. Roll the ribs individually to coat them in the seasoned flour. Then, in a pan, add a little oil and when hot add the ribs, a couple at a time, and brown them off on both sides. This sears the meat and keeps the insides nice and juicy. When you have all the ribs browned off, set them aside.

In a large pot or ovenproof casserole dish, add the olive oil, the onion and a pinch of salt and pepper, and fry until browned and softened (this should take about 7 minutes). Then add in the crushed garlic and the tomato puree and cook for another minute or two, stirring all the time. Add the Guinness and 400mls of the chicken stock, the thyme and the rosemary sprigs. Bring this to a boil and then simmer and add the ribs to the pot.

Pop this into the oven (with a tight-fitting lid on) and cook low and slow for around 3 hours, until the meat is falling off the bone.

Prep your fries by peeling and cutting your potatoes, and set aside in cold water, ready for frying.

While the ribs are in the oven, we'll make a roux. In a small saucepan over a medium heat, add the butter until melted, then whisk in the flour and cook, stirring all the time with a wooden spoon, for about 2 minutes, to make sure the flour cooks out. When done, set aside.

When the ribs are done, remove them from the casserole dish, set aside, and discard the herbs. You might need to skim off some of the fat from the braising liquid (if there's a skin of fat, remove it, but it depends on the meat you're using). Put your casserole dish back on the heat on the stove and add a little more chicken stock (about 100 ml) and bring to a simmer. Then whisk in the roux we made earlier, and slowly but surely a beautiful gravy will appear before your very eyes. This should take about 10–15 minutes. Whisk it every so often until you're happy with the consistency. If it's gone too thick, add a little more chicken stock.

While this is bubbling away, shred all the meat from the rib bones, add the meat to the gravy, and stir through. Check for seasoning, and add salt and pepper to taste.

To cook your fries, heat your oil to 180°C, and when ready drop your fries into your deep fat fryer and cook until golden and crispy. Alternatively, you could heat 500mls of vegetable oil in a saucepan, over a medium heat, to 160 °C, and deep fry them this way.

To assemble, get a serving dish, add a portion of fries, sprinkle your cheese on, and then spoon a healthy portion of your beef and gravy over the top. Garnish with a little fresh parsley

MONKFISH TACOS

WITH MANGO SALSA AND A CHILLI CRÈME

One of the great pleasures of taking part in Celebrity MasterChef *was getting to meet some great people, who also turned out to be great cooks. One of those was Mundy, the uber-talented singer-songwriter from Co. Offaly. In one of the early rounds, he showed the rest of us that he was a serious player in the competition when he cooked a plate of tuna tacos, complete with his own home-made taco shells. The judges almost cried as they ate them, they were that good. There was barely a bite left by the time the cameras had stopped filming their critique of Mundy's dish, but thankfully I managed to dive in and grab a morsel. They were unreal. This recipe is in honour of you, Mundy. And for the record, you still haven't sent me the recipe for your taco dish. Someday, pal, someday . . .*

SERVES 4

FOR THE MONKFISH TACOS:
- 500 G MONKFISH
- 2 TBSP RAPESEED OIL
- JUICE OF 1 LIME
- 1 TBSP CHILLI POWDER
- 1 JALAPEÑO PEPPER, CHOPPED
- 1 BUNCH OF FRESH CORIANDER, CHOPPED
- 8 FRESH TORTILLAS
- ¼ WHITE CABBAGE, SHREDDED

FOR THE SALSA:
- 1 RED ONION, FINELY DICED
- 1 BUNCH OF FRESH CORIANDER, CHOPPED
- 1 MANGO, FINELY DICED
- ZEST AND JUICE OF 2 LIMES
- 1 TOMATO, DESEEDED AND DICED
- 2 GARLIC CLOVES, CRUSHED
- RAPESEED OIL
- SALT AND PEPPER

FOR THE CHILLI CRÈME:
- 100 G SOUR CREAM
- 1 RED CHILLI, DESEEDED (IF YOU DON'T WANT IT HOT) AND FINELY DICED

Let's start with the fish. Place fish in a medium-sized dish. Whisk together the oil, lime juice, chilli powder, jalapeño and coriander, and pour over the fish. Let this marinate for 15 to 20 minutes.

Heat a pan and add a little rapeseed oil. Remove the fish from the marinade and place in the hot pan. Cook the fish for 4 minutes on the first side and then flip over and cook for another 3 minutes. Take the fish out of the pan and let it rest for 5 minutes.

On to the salsa. In a bowl, mix the red onion, chopped coriander, diced mango, lime juice, tomato and crushed garlic, and loosen with a little rapeseed oil. Season with salt and pepper to taste.

In the same pan we cooked the fish in, place the tortillas (one at a time) to heat for about 30 seconds.

To serve, slice the fish, place it into your tortilla, add a little of the shredded cabbage and drizzle the salsa over the top.

Add the diced red chilli to the sour cream, then drop a dollop of the chilli crème on the side of the tacos, and away you go . . .

DELANEY'S HOME-MADE PIZZAS

●●

One of the cooking rituals that takes place in our house is when we make our own pizzas. It normally starts on the Monday or Tuesday of any given week, when I'll text my brother Dave and ask him if Denis (my nephew) fancies coming over at the weekend to make pizzas. Dave will text back and say that he's asked Denis and that he's already jumping up and down at the prospect of them. So on a Saturday, after I've come home from work, I'll make the dough and prep the (large) variety of toppings that will sit on the pizzas. There's so much choice: meats, vegetables, cheeses, and even eggs – yes, eggs! My sister Sarah loves an egg on her pizza. I know, but I love her, and as it turns out, I love an egg on there too!

So, having made the dough, we'll roll the pizza bases out, and then it's almost processional as each of the kids (and there are quite a few) will be called over and asked what toppings they want, which they'll then spread on their pizza, and into the oven it goes. They used to stand on a step to do this, but not any more! Seven or eight minutes later, silence descends as the kids tuck into their own creations. Ten minutes later the house returns to the normal madness: picture a circus where all of the performers have been given coffee, chocolate and brown sauce. Yep, it's a quiet place to spend a Saturday afternoon . . .

SERVES 6-8

FOR THE PIZZA DOUGH:
• 2 X 7 G SACHETS DRIED YEAST
• 470 ML LUKEWARM WATER
• 1 TBSP GOLDEN CASTER SUGAR
• 800 G STRONG FLOUR
• 200 G GROUND SEMOLINA FLOUR
• 1 TSP FINE SEA SALT

FOR THE PIZZA SAUCE:
• 1 TBSP OLIVE OIL
• 1 GARLIC CLOVE, FINELY SLICED
• 1 X 400 G TIN OF CHOPPED TOMATOES
• A HANDFUL OF FRESH BASIL LEAVES
• SALT AND PEPPER, TO SEASON

Let's get the dough made. This process used to fill me with dread: I'm not a fan of baking and used to avoid doing this at all costs. But having done it once, I realised how simple it was, and how much better the taste was from a pizza base made from scratch, so it's now the only way we go in our house when it comes to pizza! The first thing to do is to get the yeast working, so add the two sachets of yeast to the lukewarm water, add in the sugar, then stir together and let it sit for 5 or so minutes.

Now, pop the flours onto on a clean surface and make a well in the centre. Then add the yeast mixture slowly, bit by bit, and mix in. It's best to go gently at this stage, using your fingers, until all of the liquid is added in. Of course the mix will look and feel stodgy, but keep at it until the dough comes together. Then the kneading can begin. This is the bit I love. Start by patting the dough into a ball, and then flour your surface (I use some of the semolina flour for this) and start kneading the dough. Push the dough away from you while holding on to the bottom, and then fold it back and repeat the process. The idea is to stretch the dough, activate the yeast and give your dough a nice elasticity. The kneading should continue for about ten minutes. Think of it as a mini workout!

You'll know the dough is done when it's nice and smooth and feels a little springy. Pop the dough into a large bowl, sprinkle some flour over it and then cover it with clingfilm and let it rest for a good half hour. After the dough is rested, cut the dough into even portions. Depending on what size of pizzas you want, this mixture should make 6 to 8 decent-size ones. Flour your surface and roll each portion of dough out to a nice thin base, and lay them on some oiled tinfoil (so they don't stick) and leave them until you're ready to add the toppings.

The pizza sauce couldn't be simpler. In a small saucepan add a little olive oil, bring to a low heat, and add the finely sliced garlic. Keep an eye on this, as you don't want the garlic to burn and go bitter. As soon as you see the garlic start to take on some colour, add the tomatoes and stir through, then add about half of the handful of the basil and stir through again, and add salt and pepper to taste. Cook this on a low heat for about 25 minutes, and then let it cool. Using a hand blender, blitz the sauce until smooth, and leave aside until needed.

Preheat your oven to 240°C.

To make up your pizzas, add a spoon of sauce to the base and spread so it covers the whole pizza. Then fill your boots with whatever toppings take your fancy. My personal favourites are serrano ham, pepperoni, red and yellow peppers, red onions, mushrooms, buffalo mozzarella (which you tear apart and dot across the pizza) and some grated Cheddar cheese. Oh, and the egg. If you want an egg, simply crack it onto the middle of the pizza.

Pop into the oven and cook for about 8 minutes. Happy days.

BRAISED LAMB SHANKS
WITH DAUPHINOISE POTATOES

●●●

This was probably the first dish that I learned to cook properly and the first dish that I cooked for dinner guests at home. I went the whole hog: I made the lamb shanks and served them with baby carrots glazed in orange juice and a blitzed pea puree. Delish. And it went down a treat. I've adapted the recipe over the years, and now find that what I've written below is the best Sunday family dinner in my repertoire. Lamb is by far my favourite meat, and this recipe can also be used for cooking a leg of lamb, or a nice leg of mutton: same ingredients, same cooking process. This is also the first recipe that I ever wrote down into my recipe book at home. It's page one. Lots of recipes have followed, but I reckon this is the one that I've cooked most often over the years. Try it, and I think you'll see why.

SERVES 4

FOR THE LAMB:
- 4 LAMB SHANKS
- 8 TBSP PLAIN FLOUR
- 2 TBSP OLIVE OIL

FOR THE GRAVY:
- 1 ONION, ROUGHLY CHOPPED
- 2 CARROTS, ROUGHLY CHOPPED
- 4 GARLIC CLOVES
- 2 TBSP PLAIN FLOUR
- 1 TBSP TOMATO PURÉE
- 3 BAY LEAVES (FRESH OR DRIED)
- A HANDFUL OF FRESH ROSEMARY, TORN INTO SPRIGS
- 350 ML RED WINE
- 500 ML LAMB STOCK

FOR THE DAUPHINOISE (SERVES 6 TO 8!):
- 500 ML MILK
- 500 ML DOUBLE CREAM
- 2 LARGE GARLIC CLOVES
- 8 LARGE MARIS PIPER OR ROOSTER POTATOES
- 100 G CHEESE OF YOUR CHOICE (I LIKE EITHER GRUYÈRE OR EMMENTHAL), GRATED

Preheat your oven to 180°C.

Let's start with prepping the lamb. Grab a large resealable food bag and pop the 8 tablespoons of flour in and season with salt and pepper. In a large frying pan, add a little olive oil and heat until very hot. We're going to sear the lamb, so pop each of the shanks into the food bag and pat until they're covered with the seasoned flour. When the oil in the pan is hot, place one shank in and brown on all sides: this should take about 5 minutes. Repeat the process with all of the shanks, and then set aside until needed.

Next we'll start to build the gravy for the dish, so, in a roasting dish, add a little olive oil and pop this on top of your hob and gently heat. Then add the onion and carrots and cook for about 5 minutes. Crush the garlic (you can leave it in the skin) and add this to the onion and carrot, and cook for a further 5 minutes. Then add the 2 tablespoons of plain flour and stir through (this will help thicken the gravy on the finished dish). Add the tomato puree, then the bay leaves and a couple of sprigs of the rosemary and stir through. Finally, add the red wine and the lamb stock and stir.

Then get your lamb shanks. Score little holes in the skin and add a little of the rosemary to each hole (chop the sprigs to an inch or two in length so you can slide a sprig into each hole), and then place the four shanks on top of the carrots and onions mix. Try and stand the shanks up as opposed to lying them down on their sides, as this will give the shanks a lovely colour when cooked. Cover the tray with tinfoil and make sure you have sealed the tray all the way around. If you don't seal the tray properly, the cooking liquor will all cook off and you'll be left with no gravy, and we don't want that! Pop into the oven and cook for three hours.

In the meantime, let's crack on with the potatoes. In a large saucepan, add the cream, milk and the garlic and bring to a simmer. Prep the potatoes by slicing them really thin, to about 3 or 4 mm, which is best achieved by using a mandolin – not the stringed musical instrument, but the Japanese cooking tool that has taken many a layer of skin off chefs, particularly TV chefs: Rick Stein, to name but one. So be careful! When sliced, add the potatoes to the cream and milk, and simmer for about 3–4 minutes, until cooked. Keep an eye on the potatoes and stir them occasionally so they don't stick to the bottom of the saucepan.

Grab a large ovenproof dish and then remove the potatoes from the cream and milk and layer them into the dish. You can discard the garlic. Then pour the cream and milk mix over the potatoes, just so the mix covers the spuds. Then sprinkle the grated cheese over the potatoes and bake for 35 minutes in the oven with the lamb. When the lamb is cooked, remove and let it rest for 10 to 15 minutes. Using a hand blender, blitz the remaining cooking liquor until you have a thick, shiny, dark gravy.

I like to serve this with simple green beans or peas. To serve, spoon a portion of the potatoes onto a plate, stand one of the lamb shanks beside them, add your greens, and spoon some of that liquid gold over the lamb to finish.

SANDWICHES

"There are sandwich shops in New York which offer the nobility and gentry a choice of no less than 100 different sandwiches, all of them alluring and some of them downright masterpieces."

— H.L. MENCKEN

"My weaknesses have always been food and men — in that order."

— DOLLY PARTON

Who hasn't dreamed of standing in an authentic NYC diner, in a long line, waiting to put your order in for the sandwich of your choice? The anticipation, the smells, the noise . . . If, like me, you change your mind in a queue about eight times before you get to the top and order, I've tried to narrow down your selection here by keeping it to ten: ten sandwiches that take you across the States, from NYC to Miami, from New Orleans to California. The classic of all deli classics is in here too: the Reuben. What a sandwich. It was my introduction to the sandwich counter at a NYC diner. I wasn't that hungry and thought I'd just have a sandwich so I wouldn't spoil my appetite for dinner that night. Boy, did I get that wrong! Arriving on a large plate, there was the Reuben. I managed half of it. And then went back to the hotel and slept for three hours. Happily I woke in time for dinner . . .

THE NEW ORLEANS MUFFULETTA

●●

This sandwich originated with Italian immigrants who arrived in the port of New Orleans, Louisiana, between 1800 and 1900. In the area of the city that was to become known as Little Palermo, several Sicilian bakeries sprung up and brought with them the traditional Sicilian loaf called the muffuletta. A muffuletta is a large, round, flattened loaf with a sturdy texture. It's nigh on impossible to get your hands on in the Emerald Isle, so for this recipe I've gone for a focaccia loaf, tipping my mythical cap to the Italian influence on this sandwich. You can choose your favourite types of Italian deli meats for the sandwich. The same goes for the cheese, but to keep it traditional, make the olive mix and go with provolone or Swiss cheese.

SERVES 4-6

- 255 G MIXED OLIVES IN OIL
- 1 TBSP CAPERS
- 85G ROASTED RED PEPPERS, CHOPPED
- 2 TBSP FRESH PARSLEY, CHOPPED
- 1 GARLIC CLOVE, CRUSHED
- 3 TBSP EXTRA VIRGIN OLIVE OIL
- 1 TBSP RED WINE VINEGAR
- 1 LARGE FOCACCIA LOAF OF YOUR CHOICE
- 4 SLICES SALAMI
- 4 SLICES PROSCIUTTO
- 4 SLICES MORTADELLA
- 4 SLICES PROVOLONE CHEESE

We'll start by making the filling for the sandwich. In a food processor, add the olives, capers, peppers, parsley and garlic. Pulse this mixture until you end up with a breadcrumb-consistency mix; you don't want it extra smooth, so leave a few lumps in there to give a real crunch and texture to the sandwich. Pop the mixture into a large bowl, add the olive oil and vinegar and mix through. If you have the time and the patience, let this mix sit for as long as you can (preferably overnight) before assembling the sandwiches.

Cut your loaf in half (so you end up with a top and bottom, like a traditional sandwich) and spread the olive mixture on each slice, including the oil from the mixture, as this will soak into your bread. Add your meats and cheeses, and enjoy!

THE MONTE CRISTO

●●●

This is the American version of that classic French sandwich, the croque-monsieur. It's also the American version of the staple of every Irish lunchbox since the '60s, the ould ham and cheese sambo! Now, if you fancy mixing this up a little, replace the ham with turkey, and you can also change the cheese to the cheese of your liking, but for me the gouda is perfect for this, as it will melt really well and is a beautiful creamy counter to the salty ham. Yum.

SERVES 1

- 3 SLICES OF A GOOD WHITE SANDWICH BREAD
- 2 TBSP DIJON MUSTARD
- 2 TSP MAYONNAISE
- 3 SLICES HAM
- 3 SLICES GOUDA
- 1 FREE-RANGE EGG
- 2 TBSP MILK
- 1 TSP PAPRIKA
- SALT AND PEPPER, TO SEASON
- 3 TBSP BUTTER

Let's prep the bread so it's ready to receive all that meaty, cheesy goodness. Cut the crusts off bread. Arrange the three slices on a board and brush two with a spoon of mustard, and one with a spoon of mayonnaise (this is the slice that we'll use as the middle of the sandwich).

Now layer the sandwich. Lay your ham on slice number one and then add a slice of the Gouda cheese. Pop the middle slice on (the one with the mayo), then add second slices of ham and cheese. Pop the top slice on. Now, for me, you have to flatten the sandwich down so that when you pop it into the pan it'll get a nice colour all over as it cooks. Sit a chopping board on the sandwich for a couple of minutes: this will do the trick.

Now, in a bowl, mix together the egg, the milk, the paprika, and a pinch of salt and pepper. Dip your sandwich into the mix and cover well on both sides.

In a pan, on a medium heat, melt the butter and pop the sandwich in and cook for about 4 minutes per side. The sandwich will turn a beautiful golden colour. To keep things neat and tidy, sear off the edges for a couple of seconds before removing to a cutting board to slice. Some diners will serve this with a relish on the side to dip your sandwich into, and some will give the sandwich a light dusting of powdered sugar, but honestly I don't think you don't need to serve anything with this: it's a winner all on its own!

THE PILGRIM

●●

This sandwich is one of the most popular in the US. It's traditionally made the day after Thanksgiving and is seen as the perfect way to use up all that leftover turkey and stuffing. But rather than have to wait until St Stephen's Day, I've replaced the turkey with chicken so you can use this recipe the day after your latest roast chicken dinner. I've also added in my stuffing recipe, which I use for my regular Sunday roasts, and for the Christmas turkey. Like a lot of things, it's even better the day after.

SERVES 4

- 4 NICE SOFT WHITE BREAD ROLLS OR BRIOCHE BUNS
- 50 G BUTTER
- 100 G MAYONNAISE
- 180 G PACK OF CREAM CHEESE
- 8 SLICES OF CHICKEN, LEFTOVER FROM THE SUNDAY ROAST OR FROM THE DELI COUNTER
- 8 SLICES OF A GOOD SHARP IRISH CHEDDAR CHEESE
- 310 G CRANBERRY SAUCE
- 250 G STUFFING (SEE SIDES, P. 214)
- 1 HEAD OF COS OR ROMAINE LETTUCE

I like to start by toasting my buns (feel free to add a joke here). So, cut your buns, spread a little butter on them, and in a hot pan (with no oil) pop them in butter side down and cook for a couple of minutes. The butter will go a beautiful golden colour.

To assemble the sandwich, start by spreading some mayonnaise on one side of the bun and cream cheese on the other, then add your chicken, followed by a couple of slices of cheese. Leaving the sandwich open, pop the half with the cheese under the grill for a minute or two and let the cheese melt slightly. Then take it out of the grill, add your cranberry sauce and a layer of the stuffing, and finish off with lettuce. Pop the other bun with the cream cheese on it back on top, and that's that.

Slice the buns and serve with a couple of pickles on the side. When you bite into this sandwich you get the crunch from the lettuce, the soft stuffing, the sweet cranberry sauce and that tasty chicken.

THE REUBEN

● ●

No diner cookbook would be complete without a Reuben. No trip to NYC would be complete without a Reuben. Before I'd ever set foot in the US, I knew that if and when I ever got there, this sandwich was top of my list of things to experience. So when the moment arrived in a deli in NYC, I ordered my Reuben and was amazed by what was presented to me: a sandwich that stood about six inches tall, with half a pound of hot pastrami, half a pound of hot corned beef, sauerkraut and Swiss cheese, all topped off with a Russian dressing, and crammed between two soft slices of rye bread. They say never meet your heroes, as you'll ultimately be disappointed. Well, that day, I wasn't. It's an amazing sandwich that I've tried to replicate here. I've put rye bread in the recipe, but it can be hard to find, so feel free to use the bread of your choice. The corned beef that we use in this recipe is the same we use in our corned beef hash recipe (see p. 210), so you're getting two dishes from the same cut of meat. Enjoy!

SERVES 4

FOR THE RUSSIAN DRESSING:
- 1 TBSP ONION, FINELY CHOPPED
- 340 G MAYONNAISE
- 85 G CHILLI SAUCE OR KETCHUP
- 2 TSP HORSERADISH SAUCE
- 1 TSP HOT SAUCE
- 1 TSP WORCESTERSHIRE SAUCE
- ¼ TSP SWEET PAPRIKA
- SEA SALT

FOR THE SANDWICH:
- 50 G BUTTER
- 8 SLICES RYE BREAD
- 8 SLICES SWISS CHEESE
- 8 SLICES CORNED BEEF
- 8 SLICES PASTRAMI
- 450 G SAUERKRAUT

We'll start with the Russian dressing, which is also known as Thousand Island dressing. So, with a mortar and pestle, mash the onion to create a paste, then pop this into a bowl with the mayo, the chilli sauce, the horseradish sauce, the Worcestershire sauce, the hot sauce (as much or as little as you like!) and the sweet paprika, and whisk together. Season with salt to taste. This is a great side dip too and can be used with fries, burgers and such.

So on to the sandwich. Heat a little butter in a pan and pop the slices of bread in side by side. After a couple of minutes, while the slices are still in the pan, lay the Swiss cheese on the bread and let it melt slightly. Remove the bread from the pan and put some of the dressing on both slices. Then layer on the corned beef, followed by the pastrami, then the sauerkraut. Put the sandwich together. If you like, you can pop it back into the pan to further melt the cheese. Serve by slicing down the middle, and pop a pickle on the side!

THE CLASSIC PATTY MELT

● ●

This recipe finally bridges the gap between a burger and a sandwich: the patty melt. This is another recipe where you can call the shots in terms of what type of bread you use. I find that a good white sandwich bread is great for this, but you can go down the grain route, or even try a thin panini. I like to serve this with a Thousand Island or Russian dressing, but again, feel free to replace this with ketchup, mayonnaise or a hot sauce, if that's your thing! The key to this sandwich is the beef: get this right and you're on a winner. If you're in your butcher's, ask them for a ground beef that's 80/20, which means it's 80 per cent lean. This is also a good rule of thumb for beef that you're going to use for burgers.

SERVES 4

FOR THE CARAMELISED ONIONS:
- 2 TBSP OLIVE OIL
- 2 LARGE WHITE ONIONS, FINELY SLICED

FOR THE PATTY MELTS:
- 480 G FRESHLY GROUND BEEF, PREFERABLY CHUCK
- 1 TBSP ONION POWDER
- 1 TSP FRESHLY GROUND BLACK PEPPER
- 1 TSP SALT
- 8 SLICES BREAD
- 170 G THOUSAND ISLAND DRESSING (SEE P. 122)
- 8 SLICES RED IRISH CHEDDAR CHEESE
- 2 TBSP UNSALTED BUTTER

The first job is to get the caramelised onions done. So, in a pan, add the olive oil on a medium heat and add the finely sliced onions. You want to give these a good cook, to get the onions softened and turned a nice brown colour. This should take about 15 minutes.

For the patties, grab a large bowl and mix the ground beef with the onion powder and pepper. Give these a thorough mix, and divide into four portions. Using your hands, form into burger patty shapes. Then, on a medium-high heat, add a little oil to a pan and pop the patties in. Cook them for about 3 minutes until you have a nice crust on the bottom and then gently flip them over and cook on the other side for the same amount of time. Just keep an eye on them and check to see when they're cooked to your liking. When done, leave to rest.

To assemble the sandwich, spread some of the Thousand Island dressing on each slice of bread, then add a patty, two slices of the good Irish Cheddar cheese and finally the caramelised onions. In a warm pan add a little butter and lay the sandwich into the pan. Press down with a spatula and fry until a nice golden-brown colour, then flip them over and do the same on the other side.

Slice the sandwich and serve with dressing on the side.

"Donuts: is there anything they can't do?"

— HOMER SIMPSON

"Everything you see I owe to spaghetti."

— SOPHIA LOREN

THE GRILLED PORTOBELLO BAGEL

WITH SMOKED TOMATO RELISH

●●●●●●●●●●●●●●●●●●●●●●●●●●●●●●●●●●●●●●

On a recent trip to LA, I was contacted by a friend and arranged to meet him for lunch. We were to meet in a diner that he suggested. 'Wait till you taste the food, man, it's amazing,' he told me over the phone that morning, sounding very excited. You know what it's like: you've found a great eatery and you can't wait to share it with your friends. I put the address in the satnav and off I went. I met my pal, and we entered the diner, which was buzzing. 'Happy days,' I thought. Then I looked at what the folks were eating. I then looked at the menu on the wall above the counter. Yep. It was a vegetarian diner. My heart sank, as I'd had visions of myself tucking in to a burger, or a plate of corned beef hash, but no. No hash. No burger. I did, however, spot something I liked on the menu. Portobello mushrooms. 'Right. I'll give this a go,' I thought. I ordered this bagel, and devoured it. The combination of those big meaty mushrooms and that smoked relish was amazing. I was a happy camper, and I left with a full belly and a clear conscience.

SERVES 4

FOR THE BAGEL AND MUSHROOMS:
· 8 PORTOBELLO MUSHROOMS
· 2 GARLIC CLOVES, FINELY SLICED
· 100 ML OLIVE OIL
· A SPLASH OF BALSAMIC VINEGAR
· 4 BAGELS
· 100 G FRESH THYME
· 1 PACK OF WASHED BABY SPINACH

FOR THE SMOKED TOMATO RELISH:
· 75 ML SMOKED OIL
· ½ RED ONION, FINELY DICED
· 2 GARLIC CLOVES, CRUSHED
· 2 TSP SUGAR
· 1 TSP RED WINE VINEGAR
· 2 PUNNETS CHERRY TOMATOES, CUT IN HALF
· SALT AND PEPPER, FOR SEASONING

Preheat your oven to 160°C.

The first thing to do is to clean the mushrooms. Just get a pastry brush and clean off any dirt that might be on them. Don't wash them, as they will retain the water! A little care and attention is all that's needed, and if you need to peel off little sections, go for it. Grab a baking tray, put some greaseproof paper on it, and lay the mushrooms on. Divide the finely sliced garlic and the thyme between each of the mushrooms and lay some on top of them. Season the mushrooms well, give each of them a glug of olive oil and a splash of the balsamic vinegar, and then pop them into the oven to cook for about 12 minutes. When done, remove from the oven, and keep hot.

To make the tangy smoked tomato relish, grab a saucepan and, over a medium heat, add the smoked oil.

Add the onions and allow them to soften on a medium heat; this will take about 10 minutes. When the onions are soft, add the crushed garlic, the sugar and the vinegar, and mix through. Then add the tomatoes. Season well with salt and pepper. Allow this to cook away gently on a low heat for about 15 minutes.

To serve, toast the bagels, then cover them with a little drizzle of olive oil. Layer on some of the spinach, then pop two mushrooms on each bagel and two spoonfuls of the tomato relish on top. Pop the other half of the bagel on and you're done!

THE MOJO PORK SPECIAL

● ●

This is a sandwich that goes a long way. It's also a sandwich that takes a little time to get the best results – we marinate the meat and leave it overnight – and it's so worth the effort, believe me! I've designed this recipe to make enough for seven or eight sandwiches, so this is one that is ideal if you're having a picnic or having some friends and family over to the house. This is one to share. Also, the recipe and method for making our mojo pork can then be used in other dishes: for example, in our Cubano sandwich (see p. 131) we can use this pork. This sandwich has a little kick, but nothing too hot; I'm using various spices in the rub and marinade that will mellow as they're doing their work. When you've made this mojo pork, you'll have opened a door to numerous dishes, both hot and cold, and filled with flavour. Like all of the sandwiches here, feel free to use the bread of your choice. The choices are endless, but for me it's got to be sourdough.

SERVES 6-8

- 1 PIECE OF PORK LOIN, APPROX. 2 KG
- 100 G UNSALTED BUTTER
- 1 SOURDOUGH LOAF

FOR THE MOJO RUB:
- 2 TBSP CUMIN SEEDS
- 3 TBSP WHOLE BLACK PEPPERCORNS
- 1 TBSP CORIANDER SEEDS
- 2 TBSP SOFT BROWN SUGAR
- 1½ TSP SEA SALT

FOR THE MARINADE:
- 400 ML OLIVE OIL
- 200 G JALAPEÑO CHILLIES
- 12 GARLIC CLOVES, CRUSHED
- 1 TSP SALT
- 1 TSP GROUND BLACK PEPPER
- 250 ML FRESH LIME JUICE (ABOUT 10 LIMES)
- 1 BUNCH OF FRESH CORIANDER, CHOPPED
- 3 TBSP CIDER VINEGAR

To start, let's get the rub made. In a pestle and mortar add all rub ingredients and grind until it reaches a coarse powder texture. This mix will make about 8 tablespoons of the rub, but we'll only need 2 or 3 tablespoons for this recipe, so pop the rest into an airtight container and save for future use. Put your pork loin into a large food bag along with the 2–3 tablespoons of your rub and coat the piece of meat thoroughly. Pop this into the fridge while we make the marinade.

For the marinade, place all the marinade ingredients into your food processor and blend until you have the consistency of a pesto. Remove the pork from the fridge, but leave it in the bag and add in the marinade so it covers the meat. Seal the bag again, place back into the fridge, and leave overnight.

Preheat the oven to 175°C. Remove the pork from the marinade, let it get to room temperature, and place on an ovenproof tray, discarding the marinade. (If you leave the marinade on while cooking, you could make the piece of meat slightly bitter.) Place the tray on the middle shelf of the oven and cook for an hour and twenty minutes. Check after this time with a meat thermometer, and you're looking for a temperature of 70°C. If it's under 70°C, give it another ten minutes.

Remove the meat from the oven, and set aside to rest. Keep the roasting tray, as we'll use these cooking juices later, but first add 100 g of butter to the tray, and allow it to melt and deglaze the tray. Add the resting juices from the pork into this as well. When the liquor is cooled, pass through a sieve into a little jug. You're going to use this to butter the sliced sourdough loaf.

To serve, slice the loaf into generous slices, coat with the melted butter, slice the pork thinly and layer onto the bread. You can add a variety of garnishes, like chutneys, pickles.

This is a sandwich that takes time to make, but boy will your guests be happy.

THE CUBANO

●●●

One of the joys of writing this book was doing the research. I've discovered more about certain foods, ingredients and cooking styles than I ever imagined. While researching this sandwich (a sentence I never thought I'd use in my life), I came across this story. It describes the origins of 'Cuban bread' that was originally used in the Cubano sandwich. Back in 1896, in Ybor City in Tampa, Florida, a Sicilian-born baker named Francisco Ferlita was the first to bake Cuban bread, which typically was a loaf that measured three feet long. A loaf cost three to five cents, and it was so popular that it was delivered every morning like milk. Houses in Ybor City often had a sturdy nail driven into the door frame on the front porch, and a bread deliveryman would impale the fresh loaf of bread on the nail before dawn. I love the thought of that. And I love the idea of sneaking down the stairs at first light, taking a few sneaky bites and then blaming the birds when your parents wondered why two cents' worth of their loaf was missing. I've chosen to use a sourdough loaf in this recipe, as this is my go-to bread when I'm in a diner, but if you want to go authentic and make a Cuban loaf, it's a simple white bread recipe that generally includes a small amount of fat in the form of lard or vegetable shortening. This sandwich is described as the Cuban version of a ham and cheese sandwich, and who doesn't love a ham and cheese sandwich!

SERVES 3

- 50 G BUTTER, MELTED
- 1 SOURDOUGH LOAF (USE 2 SLICES PER PERSON)
- 50 G DIJON MUSTARD
- 6 SLICES MOJO PORK (SEE P. 129)
- 6 SLICES CHEDDAR OR THE CHEESE OF YOUR CHOICE
- 3 GHERKINS, THINLY SLICED
- 6 SLICES PASTRAMI

Preheat your grill to a high heat.

In a small pot, melt the butter. While still warm, brush both sides of each slice of your bread. Heat a small frying pan on a medium heat, and put a small drop of olive oil in. When hot, place the buttered bread in the pan and let it heat through for about 30 seconds, then flip over and do the other side of the bread. It should start to get a little crispy. Take the bread off the pan and brush one side with the mustard. Then layer a slice (or two!) of the mojo pork, a slice of cheese, a couple of slices of gherkin and finally a slice (or two!) of the pastrami.

Place the sandwich (without the top on) under the grill for a couple of minutes until the cheese starts to melt, then remove and place the other slice of bread on top. You can serve this with a few fries, or with a side salad, but honestly, even on its own this is a great meal.

THE CONEY ISLAND
LOBSTER ROLLS

●●●

They say, 'If you haven't eaten a lobster roll in New England, then you haven't eaten a lobster roll.' A proud statement from the food aficionados in the US. However, we have some of the best seafood in the world on this side of the pond, including lobsters, and I reckon if any of our New England cousins tried my lobster rolls, they'd be more than happy. The Coney Island reference comes from a restaurant there called Nathan's Famous, which has been home to the world-famous frankfurter and the famous hot-dog-eating championships every year since 1916. They also did a mean lobster roll back in the day, and this is my homage to that.

SERVES 2

· 2 LOBSTER TAILS, UNCOOKED
· SALT AND PEPPER
· 1 LIME
· OLIVE OIL, FOR DRIZZLING
· 200 G CRÈME FRAICHE
· A SMALL HANDFUL OF DILL, FINELY CHOPPED
· A SMALL HANDFUL OF CHIVES, FINELY CHOPPED
· 4 SMALL HOT DOG OR SUBWAY-STYLE ROLLS

Preheat your oven to 160°C.

Pop your lobsters on a lined baking tray, and season with salt and pepper. Cut the lime in half and place on the tray, and drizzle a little olive oil over both lobster and the lime. Pop into the oven and bake for about 20 minutes.

When cooked, remove from the oven and allow to cool. Remove the lobster meat from the shells. Pour any cooking juices from the tray into a bowl, and squeeze the roasted lime halves in. Add the crème fraiche into the bowl and mix well. Add in the finely chopped dill and the chives. With the lobster picked and cut into bite-size pieces, add them to this mix, and add salt and pepper if needed.

To serve, cut the 4 rolls (not all the way through) and split the filling between them. Garnish with a little sprinkling of dill and a drizzle of the sauce.

THE BBQ PIG-CHEEK BAGEL

WITH APPLE KETCHUP

●●●

One of the best things about having a good butcher's near you is that they can recommend certain cuts of meat for certain dishes. I'm blessed with a great butcher in our village, Padraig Howley, who never fails to deliver great-quality produce. He's also the type of butcher who, when you order a certain cut of meat, will ask, 'What are you going to do with that now?'. The pig cheeks for this recipe can be prepared by your butcher – just ask them to trim them for you and they'll be ready to go. It's also a cheaper cut of meat, and because we're going to use my favourite cooking method, low and slow, it'll deliver big-time on flavour. The addition of the tasty little apple ketchup will give this sandwich a nice balance. Sweet pork and tangy apples: a marriage made in heaven – or at least in my house, twice a week.

SERVES 4

FOR THE BAGELS:
- OLIVE OIL, FOR FRYING
- 8 PIG CHEEKS, TRIMMED BY YOUR BUTCHER
- 150 ML CIDER
- 50 ML WATER
- 2 STAR ANISE
- 1 TSP MUSTARD SEEDS
- 75 ML SOY SAUCE
- 4 BAGELS

FOR THE APPLE KETCHUP:
- 3 GRANNY SMITH APPLES, PEELED AND CORED
- 85 G GRANULATED SUGAR
- 85 ML CIDER VINEGAR
- ½ A BUNCH OF FRESH BASIL
- JUICE AND ZEST OF 1 LEMON

Preheat your oven to 150°C.

Grab a big casserole dish with a lid. Put the casserole dish on a medium heat. Add a little olive oil, pop the pig cheeks in and cook on a medium heat for about 10 minutes: we're looking to brown the meat off here. When done, add the cider, the water, the star anise, the mustard seeds and the soy sauce and mix together. Pop the lid on and place in the oven. Cook this for 3 hours, low and slow.

While this is doing its thing in the oven, let's make the apple ketchup. In a small pan, heat a drop of olive oil, add the apple and let this colour a little. Then add the sugar and allow this to caramelise. When you're happy that the apples are nice and soft, add the cider vinegar and a splash of water. Cook this gently for another 10 minutes. When done, pop the mixture into a food processor and add the basil and the juice and zest of a lemon, and blend until nice and smooth. Remove and chill in a covered bowl in the fridge.

Back to the pork. When it's cooked, remove it from the casserole dish and pop it onto a plate. Put the casserole dish back on the heat and allow the cooking liquor to reduce until it becomes a nice glaze. In a bowl, break the meat up using a couple of forks and add a couple of spoonfuls of the glaze to it. Mix well and check for seasoning. Add salt and pepper to taste.

To serve, toast the bagels, fill with the pig cheek mix, and top off with a dollop of that tangy apple ketchup.

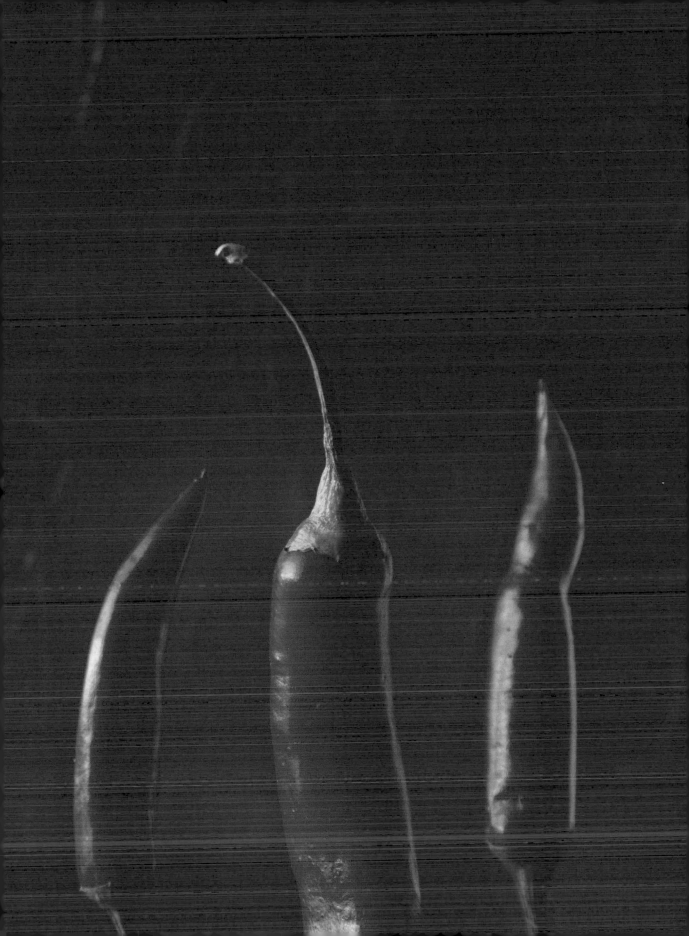

DESSERTS

"Your body is not a temple, it's an amusement park. Enjoy the ride."

— ANTHONY BOURDAIN

"My doctor told me to stop having intimate dinners for four. Unless there are three other people."

— ORSON WELLES

There's always room for dessert. It's one of the many mantras I live my life by. Whether you've pushed your way through an entire three-course meal or just fancy swinging by the diner for a cup of joe and a slice of something sweet, there's always room. One of the telltale signs of a good deli is the selection of desserts that are on offer. Something I'll always do in a diner is check the dessert menu before ordering my main. If I see my go-to diner dessert (the Key lime pie) then I know I'm in for a good meal. The desserts that I've featured in this chapter cover a range of occasions, from kids' parties (the blondie cupcakes and the milkshake) to a romantic dinner for two (the New York cheesecake and the red velvet cake) to family dinner time (the banoffee pie and the all-American apple pie). Desserts for one and all! That'd make a great campaign slogan, wouldn't it? Maybe I'll run for office, with that as my main policy. Would I get your vote? Try these recipes and let me know . . .

BLONDIE CUPCAKES

●●

Baking has never been my forte. I'm not quite sure why. It's so precise and, being a Virgo, I should excel in the exactitude of baking. But I don't. I lack that vital ingredient when it comes to baking: patience. And I hate mess too. My family will tell you I'm a bit of a Monica Geller in the kitchen; I'm washing my plate while everyone else is still eating their dinner. Whenever baking has taken place at home, it's like the house has been burgled: flour everywhere, and every pot and pan in the house used. The baker in our house is my wife Lisa, a brilliant baker, like her mam, Evelyn, and her sister Karen (who is an amazing baker!). Lisa makes gingerbread men for the boys and cakes for occasions. I eat them. That's my contribution when it comes to baking in the Delaney house. But no more! Here's a recipe I can finally make! But don't tell anybody. I'm quite happy to continue my role as 'chief taster of baked goods' in the Delaney household . . .

MAKES 16 CUPCAKES

FOR THE CUPCAKES:
- 175 G PLAIN FLOUR
- 1 TBSP BAKING POWDER
- 175 G GOLDEN CASTER SUGAR
- 175 G UNSALTED BUTTER
- 3 FREE-RANGE EGGS
- 1 TSP VANILLA EXTRACT
- 70 G WHITE CHOCOLATE CHIPS

FOR THE BUTTERCREAM:
- 200 G UNSALTED BUTTER, SOFTENED
- 400 G ICING SUGAR
- 1 TBSP ROSE WATER

FOR GARNISH:
- 50 G DARK CHOCOLATE, GRATED

Preheat your oven to 180°C.

Get your muffin tray ready and pop the muffin cases in. We'll get about 16 from this batch.

In a bowl, sift the flour and the baking powder. Meanwhile, in a mixer, beat the sugar and butter together until creamy and white. Then add the flour, the eggs (one at a time) and the vanilla extract, and keep mixing. When it's all mixed, fold in the chocolate chips.

Scoop the cake mix into the muffin cases and pop them in the oven to bake for between 15 and 20 minutes. Keep an eye on them and use a skewer to check and see if they're done. If it comes out clear, we're in the clear! When they're cooked, remove from the oven and allow to cool on a wire rack.

While the cakes are cooling, let's make the buttercream. In a bowl, beat the butter and icing sugar together until creamy and smooth and a nice white colour. Add the rose water and mix through.

To serve, pipe the butter cream on top of each of the cupcakes, and finish with a little grated chocolate!

ALL-AMERICAN APPLE PIE

●●

There are probably more versions of this recipe than any other in existence, especially in Ireland. One of my earliest food memories is standing beside the cooker at home, watching my mam make her apple tart and being given the job of stirring the pot that contained the stewing apples. That smell still takes me back. Having eaten a couple of dozen apple pies in my life, this recipe makes the best one I know of. I've watched other family members leave family gatherings with a slice or two tucked under their arm to have later on that night with a cup of tea. This is my mother-in-law's recipe. The wonderful Evelyn. I rang Evo (only we can call her that) to get the recipe and was told, 'I don't know any of the measurements, Simon, I just cook it from memory!' So, with Lisa's help, we've put her mam's recipe down on paper, for you all to enjoy. If you do, and you happen to see Evelyn on the street, stop her and tell her you loved it.

SERVES 8

FOR THE SHORTCRUST PASTRY:
· 225 G PLAIN FLOUR
· 100 G UNSALTED BUTTER, AT ROOM TEMPERATURE
· 2 TBSP MILK
· 1 TBSP WATER

FOR THE APPLE FILLING:
· 4 APPLES, PREFERABLY BRAMLEY
· 55 G CASTER SUGAR
· DROP OF WATER

Preheat your oven to 200°C.

Start by making your pastry. In a big bowl, add the flour and the butter and crumble between your fingers until mixed through. Then, in a glass, mix the milk and water and add this to the flour mix., making sure it doesn't get too wet. Roll this into a dough and let it rest for an hour.

Now on to the apples. Start by peeling and slicing the apples, not too thin – around 5mm will do. Pop these into a saucepan, and add the caster sugar and a drop of water, and let these cook down for about 15–20 minutes.

Split the dough in two and roll out to a thickness of about 5mm so that it covers the diameter of your dish. Place the first piece of rolled-out pastry onto a lined dish and bake for about ten minutes. Then remove from oven and layer the stewed apples on top, spreading them evenly. Add the second piece of rolled-out pastry on top, and sprinkle with a little caster sugar. Pop it into the oven, and cook for around 20 minutes.

Serve a slice on a plate with a nice dollop of fresh cream or a scoop of your favourite ice cream.

CHOCOLATE MALTY-EASER MILKSHAKE

●●●●●●●●●●●●●●●●●●●●●●●●●●●●●●●●●●●●●●●

A diner staple. Some would say that you can't eat a burger in a diner without having a milkshake. As a child, there's nothing better than sitting in front of a tall glass, longer than your own head, and looking at all of your favourite things crammed into that cold, creamy drink. It's not bad for an adult either. This recipe is for the king of milkshakes, the chocolate milkshake, and it is filled with (and I quote Maria von Trapp) 'a few of my favourite things . . .'

SERVES 4

· 200 G CRUSHED MALTESERS, PLUS
  EXTRA TO GARNISH
· 180 ML MILK
· 750 G GOOD CHOCOLATE ICE CREAM
· 200 ML FRESHLY WHIPPED CREAM
· 100 G MARSHMALLOWS
· 50 G POPPING CANDY

In a blender, blitz the Maltesers with a quarter of the milk. Add the ice cream and blend, slowly adding the rest of the milk bit by bit, until you get a nice smooth mixture.

Pour into a tall sundae glass and pop a scoop of whipped cream on the top. Garnish with the marshmallows, a handful of crushed Maltesers and the popping candy.

"Hors D'oeuvre: A ham sandwich cut into forty pieces."

— JACK BENNY

"You don't need a silver fork to eat good food."

— PAUL PRUDHOMME

KEY LIME PIE

●●●

This plate of loveliness gets its name from its main ingredient: small Key limes that grow throughout the Florida Keys. They are sharper than the limes you and I can get in our supermarkets. The good people of Florida take their ownership of this dish very seriously, and this is demonstrated through two events. The first was in 1965, when Florida state representative Bernie Papy Jr introduced legislation calling for a $100 fine to be levied against anyone advertising Key lime pie not made with Key limes. Strangely enough, the bill failed. Then on 1st July 2006, the Florida House of Representatives and the Florida Senate both passed legislation selecting Key lime pie as the official pie of the State of Florida. A proud moment for Floridians everywhere.

SERVES 8

· 300 G CHOCOLATE HOBNOBS
· 75 G BUTTER
· 3 MEDIUM EGG YOLKS
· 1 X 397 G TIN OF CONDENSED MILK
· ZEST AND JUICE OF 4 LIMES
· 300 ML DOUBLE CREAM
· 1 TBSP ICING SUGAR
· 50 G DARK CHOCOLATE, SHAVINGS

Preheat your oven to 160°C.

In a food processor, blitz the biscuits so that they resemble a breadcrumb texture. Pop these into a bowl.

In a small pan, melt the butter and add it to the biscuits and mix through. Pop the mixture into a 22 cm tart tin, and press it down so that it's an even thickness across the tin and up the sides. I use the back of a dessertspoon to do this. Leave aside to cool.

In a bowl, pop in the egg yolks and whisk for about 1 minute using an electric whisk. Add in the condensed milk and whisk through for another couple of minutes. Now mix in the juice and zest of the limes, and pour the mixture into your pie base. Pop back into the oven for about 15 minutes. After this, remove from the oven and chill for at least 3–4 hours, but if you can do it overnight, all the better!

To serve, carefully take the pie out of the tin and slice a generous piece onto a plate. Add the cream to the icing sugar and whisk until you have soft peaks. You can serve this cream either spread on the cake or dolloped on each individual slice. Finish the dish off by sprinkling some lime zest over the pie, and grate some of the dark chocolate on there too!

RED VELVET CAKE

* *

This is one of my favourite cakes of all time. It's the one I'll order if I see it on a diner menu. There are lots of theories about where this cake originated, some saying that it all started in the Waldorf Astoria Hotel in NYC, where the chef was very protective over his recipe. There's a great urban legend surrounding how this cake got its nickname, 'the $300 cake', and here it is:

Our friend, Dean Blair, got on a bus in San Jose one morning and shortly after, a lady got on the bus and started passing out these 3 x 5 cards with the recipe for 'Red Velvet Cake'. She said she had recently been in New York and had dinner at the Waldorf Astoria and had this cake. After she returned to San Jose, she wrote to the hotel asking for the name of the chef who had originated the cake, and if she could have the recipe. Subsequently she received the recipe in the mail, with a bill for something like $350 from the chef. She took the matter to her attorney, and he advised her that she would have to pay it because she had not enquired beforehand if there would be a charge for the service, and if so, how much would it be. Consequently, she apparently thought this would be a good way to get even with the chef.

Taken from The Vanishing Hitchhiker *by Jan Harold Brunvand (W.W. Norton & Company, 1989)*

A great story. And no, this recipe is not that one! Enjoy!

SERVES 8

FOR THE CAKE:
- 250 G PLAIN FLOUR
- PINCH OF SALT
- 1¼ TSP BICARBONATE OF SODA
- 40 G COCOA POWDER
- 240 ML VEGETABLE OIL
- 300 G GRANULATED SUGAR
- 2 LARGE FREE-RANGE EGGS
- 2 TBSP RED FOOD COLOURING
- ½ TBSP VANILLA EXTRACT
- 100 ML COFFEE, COOLED
- 240 ML BUTTERMILK
- ½ TBSP WHITE WINE VINEGAR

First things first: preheat the oven to 180°C, then grease your sandwich tins (we'll need three 8-inch tins).

In a large bowl, sift the flour, a pinch of salt, the bicarbonate of soda and the cocoa powder and set aside.

In another bowl, add the oil and the granulated sugar and, using an electric whisk, gently beat together until pale. This should take a couple of minutes. Add the eggs one at a time, and then mix in the red food colouring and the vanilla extract. Spoon in 1/3 of the sifted flour mix, and mix together.

In a jug, mix together the cooled coffee and buttermilk, and add half to the mixing bowl. Beat this in, and then beat in half of the remaining flour. Stir the white wine

FOR THE FROSTING:
- 175 G UNSALTED BUTTER, SOFTENED AND DICED
- 400 G ICING SUGAR
- 300 G CREAM CHEESE

vinegar into the remaining buttermilk and coffee mix, and pour into the cake mixture. Beat it in well, and then gently fold in the remaining flour.

Beat everything together well, then evenly divide between the three tins. Pop these into the oven and cook for 35–40 minutes. The best way to check if the cakes are cooked is to pop a skewer into the middle of the cake, and if it comes out clean, you're good to go!

When the cakes are cooked, remove them from the oven, pop them onto a wire rack and leave them to cool completely. Sometimes the cakes can be a little domed, which is all good; just slice off the domes to make the three sponges level, and keep these cutoffs for decoration later. (Or, if you're hungry, eat away!)

Now onto the cake frosting. So, in a bowl add the diced butter and, using your electric whisk again, beat until pale and creamy, which should take just a couple of minutes. Sift in the icing sugar, bit by bit, and beat it in well until smooth. Next add in the cream cheese: start with a large spoonful and beat it in, and then add the rest and beat in. This takes a little elbow grease! It'll start off looking very liquid and loose, but it'll come together and eventually appear light and whipped. Don't go to heavy on whisking: nice and easy does it! When finished, let this mixture sit in the fridge for a while to allow it to firm up a little.

So now we're ready to put the cake together. On the first sponge, drop a spoon of the frosting and spread it evenly across. Pop the second layer of sponge on and repeat, and then add the third layer and do the same again. If the frosting spills out over the edges, don't panic: just use a spatula and cover the edges with the frosting. You can go fancy and pipe the frosting on top, but to get that authentic diner feel, keep it rustic! And remember those offcuts from the cake earlier? If you've any left, sprinkle these over the finished cake. Then grab a big spoon and off you go . . .

SICILIAN CANNOLI

● ●

It's one of the most quoted lines in movie history. Allow me to paint the scene: about fifty minutes into The Godfather, just after the 'sleeps with the fishes' scene, Mafia henchmen Clemenza and Rocco get into a car with Paulie. They intend to kill him. Three shots are fired by Rocco into Paulie's head. As Rocco gets out the car, Clemenza says: 'Leave the gun – take the cannoli.' He takes the food as Paulie lies slumped against the steering wheel. Coppola gave all credit to the actor in later years: 'Richie improvised the line,' he said. Moving onto The Godfather Part III, cannoli features again, when Don Altobello is presented with a box of it as a birthday gift. They are, of course, poisoned. He dies eating the cannoli while sitting watching an opera. What a way to go.

Cannoli became an obsession for me. I couldn't wait to taste one. I'd been over to the States several times and hadn't got my hands on one, but then while on my honeymoon in Rome, I finally found it. In a small coffee shop on the back streets of Rome, I sat in wonder as the girl behind the counter placed four cannoli in a box for me. I felt like I was being given the package to deliver to Don Altobello himself. Instead, I sat outside and ate all four. The only thing that met its maker that day was this classic Italian dessert. As I said, what a way to go.

SERVES 4-5

FOR THE CANNOLI SHELLS:
- 600 G PLAIN FLOUR
- 1 TBSP CASTER SUGAR
- 75 G UNSALTED BUTTER, MELTED AND COOLED
- PINCH OF SALT
- 3 TBSP MARSALA WINE
- 1 LARGE EGG WHITE, LIGHTLY BEATEN
- 85 ML RED WINE VINEGAR
- VEGETABLE OIL, FOR FRYING

FOR THE CREAM FILLING:
- 1 KG FRESH RICOTTA CHEESE, DRAINED
- 450 G ICING SUGAR
- 1½ TSP VANILLA EXTRACT
- 110 G ORANGE PEEL, FINELY CHOPPED
- 110 G MILK CHOCOLATE CHIPS
- 110 G PISTACHIOS, FINELY CHOPPED

We'll start with the cannoli shells. Sift the flour, the salt and the sugar into a food mixer. Add the cooled melted butter and mix for a couple of minutes until it resembles a breadcrumb texture. Add the Marsala wine and the vinegar, and mix through again for another 2–3 minutes, until the dough starts to come together.

Remove the dough onto a floured surface and knead for a few minutes. Form into a ball, wrap in cling film and let it sit happily on the counter for at least an hour.

In a deep fat fryer, heat your oil to about 160°C. Alternatively, heat 500mls of vegetable oil in a saucepan, over a medium heat.

After the dough has rested, cut it into quarters. Roll each of the pieces out until it's very thin, almost to the point where you can see through it. Let these sheets sit as they are for about 5 minutes, so that they don't snap back when you cut them.

Cut circles in the dough using a 4-inch pastry cutter, and then roll each out to an oval shape. Then, using a cannoli form, which is essentially a small rolling pin, grease it with a little vegetable oil, and shape the pastry around it. You're going to wrap these, but before you do, dab a little beaten egg white on one end to form a seal.

So to the frying. Carefully drop the cannoli into the oil for less than a minute, until they go a dark golden colour and nice and crispy. Keep an eye on them. Remove the shells, drain and leave to cool completely.

For the filling, mix all of the ingredients in a bowl and then put into a piping bag. Fill one end of a cannoli with the mix, and then the other end. Repeat until they're all filled.

To serve, place two on a plate, dust with some icing sugar, and sprinkle some chocolate chips and pistachios around the plate.

BANOFFEE ETON MESS

WITH A BOURBON TWIST

●●●

There are many tales about how this dish came about. Some reports claim that it was created at a cricket match at Eton College when an over-eager Labrador sat on a picnic basket that contained a pavlova. Hence the 'mess'. Another suggests that it came from an accident in a restaurant when a chef had made a beautiful dessert, a pavlova. As he brought it to the counter to serve, it fell on the floor, but he quickly scooped it up and served it. All probably untrue, but they give us a giggle when we read them!

Normally served with strawberries, this is an easy-to-prepare crowd-pleaser. What makes this recipe easy is that I use shop-bought meringues rather than making them from scratch. My version combines the classic Eton mess components (meringues and so on) with another dessert favourite of mine, banoffee. And for those amongst us who are over eighteen, there's a little kick of bourbon in there. You're welcome, dear friends . . .

SERVES 4

- 250 ML DOUBLE CREAM
- 250 G UNSALTED BUTTER
- 250 G MUSCOVADO SUGAR
- ¾ TSP SEA SALT
- 100 ML BOURBON
- 4 SCOOPS OF CHOCOLATE ICE CREAM
- 2 MERINGUES, SHOP-BOUGHT
- 2 BANANAS, CHOPPED INTO THIN SLICES
- 2 CRUNCHIE BARS, CRUSHED
- A HANDFUL OF MARSHMALLOWS

Take half of your cream, pop it into a bowl and whisk to soft peaks. Set aside.

Now on to the delicious caramel sauce. In a saucepan, heat the butter and sugar until it starts to bubble and the sugar dissolves. When the sugar has dissolved, add the rest of your cream and stir – this will be a thick sauce – then add the salt and the bourbon, and reduce on a medium heat if necessary. Stir through and allow to cool.

To assemble the messes, get four tall glasses and start by pouring in some of the caramel sauce. Then pop in a scoop of the chocolate ice cream. Whisk the remainder of your cream to soft peaks. Crush the meringues and add these to your cream, then add the sliced bananas and the crushed Crunchie bars. Pop a scoop of this mix on top of the ice cream, and finish off with a drizzle of the caramel sauce and a sprinkle of marshmallows.

CLASSIC BAKED NEW YORK CHEESECAKE

●●

This is one of my all-time favourite desserts. I've had cheesecakes all over the world – set cheesecakes, deconstructed cheesecakes, etc. etc. – but none, and I mean none, compare with a classic baked New York cheesecake. During one of the rounds on MasterChef, we had to come up with a dessert on the spot, and straight away I made a set cheesecake. It's easier to make than the baked one, so I thought I'd have a go – I'd never made one before then. I knew when both Daniel and Robin tasted it that they wished it was a proper baked cheesecake, and it got mixed results. So this recipe is for them. I promise I'll cook it for them next time I see them. Now, this recipe takes a little time and effort and you need patience, but I promise you it'll be worth the effort.

SERVES 6-8

FOR THE CHEESECAKE BASE:
· 200 G GINGERNUT BISCUITS
· 100 G UNSALTED BUTTER, MELTED

FOR THE CHEESECAKE FILLING:
· 900 G SOFT CREAM CHEESE
· 270 G CASTER SUGAR
· ½ TSP SALT
· 70 G PLAIN FLOUR
· ZEST AND JUICE OF A LEMON
· 600 G CRÈME FRAICHE
· 1 VANILLA POD, DESEEDED
· 8 FREE-RANGE EGGS

Preheat your oven to 175°C.

This recipe will fill an 11-inch baking tin, and make sure you use a springform tin: it'll make your life a lot easier when trying to get the finished cheesecake out! Grease the bottom of the tin with a little butter or oil, and line with greaseproof paper.

Pulse the gingernut biscuits in a food processor and add the melted butter until you have a mixture similar to wet sand. Spread the mix into the tin and press down until level and firm. Cook in the oven for 15 minutes.

Make the cheesecake mix while you're waiting for the base to cook. Clean your food processor, then add everything apart from the eggs and blend. Add the eggs in one at a time and be careful not to add the next egg in until the previous one is mixed through, or your filling could split. Add all of the eggs until mixed through thoroughly.

After 15 minutes' cooking, the base should be ready, so remove from oven and up the temperature to 220°C. Pour the mix in on top of the base and place in the oven for ten minutes. After ten minutes, turn the oven down to 100°C and cook for a further 50 minutes. Turn the oven off, but leave the cheesecake in there to cool down for about an hour. Then remove it from the oven and allow it to cool completely. Put the cake into the fridge for a minimum of two hours, but overnight is best. I know it sounds like a lot of time, and believe me, the temptation to eat it straight away is huge, but have patience, my friends: good things come to those who wait.

PUMPKIN TART

●●

This is a dish that originated in North America, and is traditionally served at Halloween or on Thanksgiving. It's also a dish that has been immortalised in song, from the lofty heights of opera, featuring in Leo, the Royal Cadet *(1889) in a song called 'Farewell O Fragrant Pumpkin Pie', to the more modern classic 'Rockin' Around the Christmas Tree'.*

For me, this is a dish that goes well any time of year, and with the hints of spices and that little flick of lemon zest, it's a fresh, light tart that will keep your gang smiling.

SERVES 8

FOR THE PASTRY:
- 275 G PLAIN FLOUR
- 125 G UNSALTED BUTTER, COLD AND DICED INTO SMALL CUBES
- PINCH OF SALT
- 10 TSP COLD WATER

FOR THE FILLING:
- 1 WHOLE PUMPKIN
- 2 FREE-RANGE EGGS
- 100 G CASTER SUGAR
- 2 TSP CINNAMON
- PINCH OF NUTMEG
- 1 TSP GROUND GINGER
- 2 TSP LEMON ZEST
- 50 ML FRESH CREAM

Starting off with the pastry, sift the flour and the salt into a large bowl and add the butter. Rub the butter through the flour with your fingers until the mix resembles breadcrumbs. Add just enough water to form a nice pastry dough, and when you're happy with the consistency, form it into a small ball. Cover the bowl with some cling film and let it chill for about an hour in the fridge.

Preheat your oven to 180°C.

When the pastry has chilled, take it out, let it relax (read it a story) and then roll it out on a floured surface to about ¾ mm thick. Line a 20 cm loose-bottomed fluted fan ring. (A fluted fan ring. I love saying that. I think I enjoy typing it even more. A fluted fan ring.) Anyway, next, cover the pastry with non-stick baking paper and fill with baking beans. Pop this into the oven and cook for about 12–13 minutes. Then remove from the oven, carefully take the beans and the paper off, and return to the oven and cook for a further 5 minutes.

Now it's on to the filling. Slice the pumpkin carefully and remove the flesh by scooping it out with a large spoon. We're going to steam the pumpkin, so over a pot of water on a quiet rolling boil, pop the pumpkin flesh into a colander and steam it over the hot water. This should take about 20 minutes, until it's nice and soft. When cooked, remove and mash. Leave the mixture to cool.

Next, beat the eggs together with the sugar and stir this through the pumpkin mixture in a bowl. Add the cinnamon, the nutmeg and the ground ginger, the lemon zest and the cream, and stir through. Pour this filling into your pastry base and bake in your oven at 190°C for about 45 minutes, until the filling has set. I like to serve this with a scoop of ice cream, but you could go for a little whipped cream with some vanilla essence whisked through it.

S"MORES WHOOPIE ROUNDS

⦿⦾⦿⦾⦿⦾⦿⦾⦿⦾⦿⦾⦿⦾⦿⦾⦿⦾⦿⦾⦿⦾⦿⦾⦿⦾⦿⦾⦿⦾⦿⦾⦿⦾⦿⦾⦿⦾⦿

This is a great little dessert that will satisfy the small ones in the house. Truth be told the bigger ones will love them too! Nice and easy to make, these are a great little party dessert and, like a lot of the recipes in the book, you can put your own touch on the finished dessert. A great little twist is to sprinkle the finished cakes with popping candy, then stand back and watch the kids' faces as they take a bite and the popping begins. Also, give one to Granny and don't tell her about the popping candy. Get your phone out and film her reaction. You'll be creating a YouTube classic . . .

SERVES 6-8

· 1 PACKET OF CHOCOLATE BISCUITS, OR
  YOUR FAVOURITE BISCUITS
· 100 G 70% COCOA DARK CHOCOLATE
· 2 EGG WHITES
· PINCH OF SALT
· 100 G CASTER SUGAR

Preheat your grill to a medium heat.

Place your biscuits of choice on a cooking tray. Grate the chocolate and sprinkle it over each biscuit. In an electric mixer, whisk the egg whites with the salt until you have soft peaks, then add the sugar and continue to whisk until the mix has stiff peaks and is the consistency of a meringue.

Put the mix into a piping bag and attach a medium round nozzle. Pipe the meringue onto the biscuits in dots the size of a two-euro coin, then grill until golden-brown.

To serve, finish with some grated chocolate or popping candy. Lovely jubbly.

COCKTAILS

"In wine there is wisdom, in beer there is freedom, in water there is bacteria."

— BENJAMIN FRANKLIN

"Alcohol may be man's worst enemy but the bible says love your enemy."

— FRANK SINATRA

What better way to finish a meal than with a cocktail? It's another one of those things I love about the classic American diner. The fact that most good diners are open until the wee small hours lends itself to the fact that a staple of most good diners' menus are their cocktail lists. If you happen to find yourself in the greatest city in the world, NYC, (my opinion and I'm sticking to it) and have had a night out – maybe you've taken in a Broadway show or had stroll in Central Park (I should be working for the NYC tourist board, although they don't need my help) – why not prolong the night and find a late-night diner? Pop in, order a cocktail and do what I love to do: people watch. You'll find all sorts, at all times of the night. I remember on a recent trip to the Big Apple, I was there filming and I ended up in a diner near the hotel I was staying in, on my own, after a long night shoot. I sat at the counter and ordered a Reuben and an Old-fashioned (the drink that almost killed Don Draper). I sat and ate, and drank, while at the next table a group of NYC's finest talked about a raid they'd carried out earlier that night. I could have (and did) listen for hours. I felt like I was in an episode of *Blue Bloods* or *Hill Street Blues*. I kept checking to see if there was a camera around, because these guys were straight out of central casting: broad New Yaawwkk accents, loads of attitude and huge appetites. They re-enacted the entire raid, complete with gun noises and screams. They devoured a half-dozen chicken Parm sandwiches and a few beers, and on the way out they ordered another three sandwiches to go. 'Gotta grab somethin' for the captain!' one of them said as the waitress took the order. Brilliant. So, choose your cocktail, sit back, close your eyes, and let it take you to NYC. I recommend the Old-fashioned.

FROZEN BANANA DAIQUIRI

Without question, the most enjoyable drink I've ever had was a frozen banana daiquiri. Now, of course, it wasn't just the drink, it was the circumstances. I'll paint the picture: it's July 2005, myself and Lisa are on our honeymoon, and we've just arrived in Venice on the first leg of our grand Italian tour. We've taken the water taxi in from the airport, checked in to the hotel, and are going to hit the Venice night. Before we head out into the warm summer's air, we decide to have a drink in our hotel, in the bar at the back of the hotel to be precise, which has a terrace that faces on to one of thousands of Venetian canals. A drinks menu arrives. What to order? Will we have a cold beer? A glass of wine? Then I spot a cocktail list, and what was on top of the list? A frozen banana daiquiri. We'd never had one. So we ordered one. And then another. And, I think, another. Those couple of cocktails were the sweetest, most enjoyable drinks I've ever had. The cocktail was good, but the company was magical. Cheers . . .

• ½ LARGE BANANA, SLICED
• 50 ML LIGHT RUM
• 30 ML LIME JUICE
• 15 ML TRIPLE SEC
• 1 TSP WHITE SUGAR
• A LARGE HANDFUL OF ICE CUBES

In a blender, pop in the banana, the light rum, the lime juice, the triple sec and the sugar, and puree until nice and smooth. Add the ice cubes and blend again until slushy. To serve, pour into a cocktail glass and dress with a strip of the lime peel.

LONG ISLAND ICED TEA

●●

This was probably the first cocktail I ever tried. It sounded exotic and, indeed, it was. Some say that this is a drink that has its origins in 1972, in a bar in called the Oak Beach Inn located (unsurprisingly) in Long Island, New York. It's claimed that a barman there called Robert 'Rosebud' Butt (again, I kid you not) invented the drink as an entry into a contest to create a new mixed drink that featured triple sec. Bob Butt has his own website, where he holds firm on the claim of ownership, and I quote:

The world famous Long Island Iced Tea was first invented in 1972 by me, Robert Butt, while I was tending bar at the infamous Oak Beach Inn. I participated in a cocktail-creating contest. Triple sec had to be included, and the bottles started flying. My concoction was an immediate hit and quickly became the house drink at the Oak Beach Inn. By the mid-1970s, every bar on Long Island was serving up this innocent-looking cocktail, and by the 1980s it was known the world over.

Good man, Bob. I believe you. Cheers . . .

- 22 ML GIN
- 22 ML WHITE RUM
- 22 ML TEQUILA
- 22 ML VODKA
- 22 ML COINTREAU
- 22 ML DATE SYRUP
- 22 ML LEMON JUICE
- LEMON WEDGE
- ICE (ENOUGH TO FILL THE GLASS)
- DASH OF COCA COLA

Fill a highball glass with ice and add all the ingredients except the Coca Cola and the lemon wedge. Stir well. Top up with the Coca Cola and garnish with the lemon wedge.

THE MANHATTAN

●●●●●●●●●●●●●●●●●●●●●●●●●●●●●●●●●●●●●●●

The Manhattan: a cocktail that takes its name from my favourite place in the world. Legend has it that this cocktail got its name from the club first created it in the 1870s: the Manhattan Club in NYC. Other stories say that the drink was first made at a bar on Broadway near Houston Street by a barman named Black as far back as the 1860s. Such detail is incidental – this is a classic, pure and simple. And the first time you travel to NYC, head to a saloon bar, find a high stool and order one. That's what I did.

- ICE (ENOUGH TO FILL YOUR GLASS)
- 60 ML WHISKEY
- 1-2 DASHES OF BITTERS
- 1 STRIP OF ORANGE PEEL
- 2 CHERRIES SOAKED IN MARASCHINO LIQUEUR (IF YOU'RE A FAN OF CHERRIES THEN 3 OR 4!)
- 22 ML SWEET VERMOUTH

Place the ice in a cocktail shaker and add the whiskey, the vermouth and the bitters. Stir, don't shake. Rub the orange peel around the rim of a chilled glass, then strain in the drink. Add one or two cherries.

"There comes a time in every woman's life when the only thing that helps is a glass of champagne."

— BETTE DAVIS

"There is no bad whiskey. There are only some whiskeys that aren't as good as others."

— RAYMOND CHANDLER

THE SIMON SEZ

●●

This is a cocktail that goes by another name: the Old-fashioned. It's a classic cocktail that features bourbon, my liquor of choice. This originated in Louisville, Kentucky, as far back as 1881, in a gentlemen's club called the Pardennis Club. So proud are they of their home beverage that in 2015 Louisville named the Old-fashioned as its official cocktail.

A few years ago on a trip to NYC, while I was there filming Delivery Man *with Vince Vaughn (pardon me while I bend down and pick up that name), I was brought to a bar in Chelsea that served only bourbon cocktails. Needless to say, I sat happily at that bar for hours. However, when I stood up to leave, my legs didn't want to go. I honestly don't think it was the bourbon; I think it was the bill that did it to me.*

- 1 SUGAR CUBE
- 3 DASHES OF ANGOSTURA BITTERS
- A SPLASH OF CLUB SODA OR FLAVOURED TONIC WATER
- 1 STRIP OF ORANGE PEEL
- 1 ICE CUBE
- 60 ML BOURBON

Place the sugar cube in a whiskey glass and add the bitters. Add a splash of soda or tonic water. Add the orange peel. Crush the sugar cube with a muddler or spoon. Swirl the glass around so that the mix coats the inside of the glass. Add a cube of ice, pour over the bourbon, and serve with a stirrer.

THE BLOODY MARY

●○●○●○●○●○●○●○●○●○●○●○●○●○●○●○●○●○●

Attributed to Queen Mary I of England (known as Bloody Mary because of her penchant for executions), this is one of the best-known and best-loved cocktails in the world. An abundance of varieties of this drink exist, one better than the other depending on your personal taste and mood. Whenever I see someone ordering a Bloody Mary in a diner, I think they're either on their way out for a serious night out or on their way home from a serious night out. Whether a kick-start to your evening or a hangover cure, this is a classic.

- 50 ML VODKA
- 60 ML OF TOMATO JUICE
- 1 TSP WORCESTERSHIRE SAUCE
- 3 DASHES OF TABASCO
- ¾ TSP FRESH HORSERADISH, GRATED
- PINCH OF SALT
- PINCH OF FRESHLY GROUND BLACK PEPPER
- ICE CUBES (TO FILL YOUR GLASS)
- ¼ TSP FRESH LEMON JUICE
- 1 STALK OF CELERY
- 1 LEMON WEDGE

Grab a couple of big glasses. In one glass, add in the vodka, tomato juice, Worcestershire sauce, Tabasco, horseradish, and the salt and pepper. Top the glass up with ice. Pour the mixture into the other glass and then back into the original one. Repeat. Then pour into a separate high glass, add the lemon juice and then garnish with the celery stick and, if you fancy it, a lemon wedge.

THE MARTINI

● ●

The Martini is probably one of the most famous cocktails in the world. It's certainly one of the most talked about. There are dozens of recipes, dozens of suggestions on how to make it, what to eat with it, where to drink it, and whether or not to drink it shaken or stirred. Among the many fans of this famous cocktail are President Franklin D. Roosevelt, who favoured a 'dirty' martini (which contains a splash of olive brine or olive juice); Queen Elizabeth II, who apparently likes a 'dry' martini (made with dry white vermouth), and good old Humphrey Bogart, whose attributed last words were, 'I should never have switched from scotch to Martinis.'

Here's looking at you, kid . . .

· 15 ML DRY VERMOUTH
· 90 ML GIN
· ICE (TO FILL YOUR COCKTAIL SHAKER)
· LEMON PEEL
· 2 GREEN OLIVES

Pour the vermouth and the gin into a cocktail mixer filled with ice. Stir, don't shake. You're not James Bond. Strain the liquid into a martini glass. Squeeze the oil from the lemon peel over the top. Spear two olives onto a cocktail stick and serve on top the glass.

THE MOJITO

⦿•⦿

Among the many reasons quoted as to why or where this drink got its name, my favourite is one of the simplest: the name Mojito is simply a derivative of mojadito, *which is Spanish for 'a little wet'. I like that. It's one of those drinks, like most good cocktails, that has only a few ingredients, and it's simple to make. So, no messing around with different liquors and spices, this is how it should be made – or at least this is the way I make them!*

- ICE (ENOUGH TO FILL YOUR GLASS)
- 180 ML LIGHT RUM
- 9 SPRIGS OF MINT
- 6 TBSP FRESH LIME JUICE (ABOUT 6 LIMES)
- 4 TBSP SUGAR
- A SPLASH OF CLUB SODA
- 4 SLICES FRESH LIME

Pop the ice into a shaker and then add in the rum, 8 sprigs of the mint (torn up), the lime juice and the sugar. Shake well (give it your best Tom Cruise moves) and then serve over ice in a nice highball glass. Add a splash of the club soda. To finish, garnish with a sprig of mint and a slice of lime.

THE WHITE RUSSIAN

●●●

It always amazes me what comes into fashion and what goes. This cocktail, which was originally known as a Black Russian until some genius added cream, was up until 1998 considered to be a kind of 'meh' drink, not top of the list when it came to the great and the good ordering it. Then, in 1998, a movie came out: The Big Lebowski *by the Coen brothers, which starred Jeff Bridges as a dressing-gown-wearing, bowling-obsessed slacker, shot this drink to the top of the charts. In the movie, The Dude drinks the White Russian at every available moment; he, however, calls it a Caucasian. Since then, it's remained at the top, back where it belongs.*

- ICE (ENOUGH TO FILL YOUR GLASS)
- 60 ML VODKA
- 30 ML KAHLUA OR TIA MARIA
- 30-60 ML DOUBLE CREAM

Grab a glass and fill it with the ice. Add the Kahlua and the vodka and stir. Top up the glass with cream. If you fancy making this look like a movie star, slowly pour the cream into the drink over the back of a spoon, it'll give the drink a marbled effect.

"Stressed spelled backwards is desserts. Coincidence? I think not!"

— ANONYMOUS

"Confidence is going after Moby Dick in a rowboat and taking tartar sauce with you."

— ZIG ZIGLAR

A lot of chefs will say, 'What makes a dish is the sauce.' I agree. There's nothing that makes a Reuben sandwich better than dipping it into a tangy Russian dressing, and nothing is better on a burger than a creamy blue-cheese dressing. In this chapter I've laid out the foundations for dips and sauces that will accompany a lot of the dishes in this book, from burger toppings and salad dressings, to a classic salsa and my home-made coleslaw. Also in here you'll find the recipes for the amazing pulled pork and delicious corned beef that I use in a couple of the dishes in the book. These little side dishes will elevate your sandwich, your burger, your lunch to a different level: diner level!

HOLLANDAISE

• 2 FREE-RANGE EGG YOLKS
• 1 TSP LEMON JUICE
• 1 TSP WHITE WINE VINEGAR
• 120 G UNSALTED BUTTER, MELTED

Get a pot of boiling water on the go, and when it's boiled, turn off the heat. In a large bowl, pop in the egg yolks and add the lemon juice and the white wine vinegar and whisk until the mixture has thickened up. Pop this bowl over the pot of hot water (you might need an extra pair of hands here!) and slowly add the melted butter, whisking all the time so we form an emulsion. We're looking to get this a little less thick than mayonnaise. When done, serve immediately, and if the sauce thickens up before serving, just loosen it with a drop of hot water.

MAYONNAISE

- 1 FREE-RANGE EGG YOLK
- PINCH OF SALT
- 1 TSP WHITE WINE VINEGAR
- 1 TSP SUGAR
- 1 TSP DIJON MUSTARD
- 150 ML SUNFLOWER OIL

In a large bowl, add all the ingredients except the oil and whisk together until combined. Then add the oil very slowly as you continuously whisk the mixture. As it starts to get thicker, add the oil a little more quickly. When ready, pop into a bowl, cover and refrigerate until needed.

BLUE-CHEESE DRESSING

- 3 TBSP BUTTERMILK
- 150 G BLUE CHEESE
- 2 TBSP MAYONNAISE
- 3 TBSP SOUR CREAM
- 2 TSP WHITE WINE VINEGAR
- 1 CLOVE GARLIC, CRUSHED
- ¼ TSP SUGAR

In a bowl, start with the milk and crumble the blue cheese in. Use the back of a fork to mash the cheese into the buttermilk, and mix through. This is going to be a lumpy dressing, so don't worry about getting the mix too smooth. Add in the mayo, the sour cream, the vinegar, the crushed garlic and the sugar, and mix until well blended together. Taste, and then add salt and pepper if needed. Cover and refrigerate until required.

RANCH DRESSING

- 450 G MAYONNAISE
- 110 G CRÈME FRAICHE
- 110 ML BUTTERMILK
- 1 CLOVE GARLIC, CRUSHED
- ½ BANANA SHALLOT, VERY FINELY DICED
- ¼ TSP FRESHLY GROUND BLACK PEPPER
- PINCH OF CAYENNE PEPPER
- PINCH OF SALT
- 2 TSP CHIVES, FINELY CHOPPED
- A COUPLE OF DROPS OF WORCESTERSHIRE SAUCE

In a bowl, combine all the ingredients and mix well. This is a both a great salad dressing and a great burger topping.

SWEET CHILLI SAUCE

●●●●●●●●●●●●●●●●●●●●●●●●●●●●●●●●●●●●●●

- 350 ML WATER
- 350 ML RICE VINEGAR
- 2 TSP FRESH GINGER, GRATED
- 1 CLOVE GARLIC, CRUSHED
- 340 G SUGAR
- 2 TSP RED CHILLI, CHOPPED
- 2 TSP KETCHUP
- 1 TSP CORNFLOUR
- 1 TSP WATER

In a saucepan over a high heat, add the water and vinegar, and bring to a boil. Stir in the ginger, the garlic, the sugar, the chilli pepper and the ketchup, and lower down to a simmer. Next, add the teaspoon of cornflour to a teaspoon of water, and then add the mix into the pan and cook out for 5 to 7 minutes. When done, pop into a serving bowl, cover with cling film and pop into the fridge until required.

TOMATO SALSA

- 3 FRESH TOMATOES
- ½ RED ONION
- 2 RED CHILLIES, SEEDS REMOVED (IF YOU'RE A WUSS LIKE ME)
- JUICE OF 1 LIME
- SALT AND PEPPER
- 1–2 TBSP OLIVE OIL
- PINCH OF DRIED OREGANO
- ½ A BUNCH OF FRESH CORIANDER, CHOPPED

Prep starts with chopping. Quarter the tomatoes, de-seed them and then chop finely. Next, chop the red onion and the chillies as finely as you like. I like to give these a fine dice, but you can leave yours chunky if that's your preference. When done, put the tomatoes, onion and chillies into a large bowl, then add the rest of the ingredients and mix through well. Loosen with an extra tablespoon of oil if needed. When you're done, cover and refrigerate, and leave for a couple of hours before serving.

CORNED BEEF

(FOR THE CORNED BEEF HASH)

●●

FOR THE SPICE BLEND:
- 2 TSP GROUND CORIANDER
- 1 TSP CARAWAY SEEDS
- 1 TSP BLACK PEPPER
- 1 TSP DRIED THYME
- ¼ TSP GROUND CLOVES

FOR THE BEEF:
- 2 TBSP VEGETABLE OIL
- 1.5–2 KG PIECE OF CORNED BEEF (BRISKET)
- 6 LARGE CARROTS, PEELED AND CHOPPED
- 2 WHITE ONIONS, SLICED
- 5 GARLIC CLOVES, PEELED
- 3 BAY LEAVES
- 500 ML BEEF STOCK

Preheat your oven to 160°C.

The first job is to make up our spice blend, which we'll rub into the meat later. In a small bowl, add the coriander, the caraway, the black pepper, the thyme, and the ground cloves. Mix well and set aside.

The next job is to sear the beef. In a large frying pan, add the oil and, when hot, pop the beef in and sear on all sides. This will take a minute or two on each side, but make sure you get it all seared, as this will pay off in flavour later on!

Then, in a large casserole dish, add the carrots, the onions, the garlic and the bay leaves. Next, rub our spice blend into the beef, all over. Then pop the beef into the casserole dish on top of the veg and cover with the beef stock. Pop into the oven, and cook for at least 4 hours – the longer the better.

When ready, leave to cool a little. If you're making the corned beef hash dish, pull the meat apart using two forks. Alternatively, leave the joint whole, cook some spuds and cabbage, and you've got yourself a cracking Sunday dinner!

PULLED PORK

FOR THE PORK SHOULDER:
- 2 TBSP SMOKED PAPRIKA
- 2 TBSP GROUND CUMIN
- 2 TBSP CAYENNE PEPPER
- 2 TBSP GROUND FENNEL (IF YOU CAN ONLY GET FENNEL SEEDS, GIVE THEM A BASH IN A PESTLE AND MORTAR)
- 4 TBSP SOFT DARK BROWN SUGAR
- 100 ML CRAFT BEER
- 2.5 KG PIECE OF PORK SHOULDER

FOR THE BARBECUE SAUCE:
- 100 ML RED WINE VINEGAR
- 150 G SOFT DARK BROWN SUGAR
- 100 ML CRAFT BEER
- 200 ML TOMATO KETCHUP
- 20 ML WORCESTERSHIRE SAUCE

To make the rub, add all the spices and sugar to a bowl and mix, then add the beer and rub on to the pork shoulder. Leave to marinate overnight.

The next day, preheat the oven to 120°C. Mix all the ingredients for the barbecue sauce. Place the pork in an ovenproof dish and cover with the barbecue sauce. Cover with tinfoil and place in the middle of oven for 6 hours.

Remove from the oven and let it rest for 20 minutes. Then take the pork out of the roasting tray and pop any remaining resting juices into a pan on a medium heat, to reduce to a glaze.

Pull the meat apart with a couple of forks and add the reduced juice to coat the pork. Keep warm until needed.

COLESLAW

FOR THE COLESLAW
- 500 G CABBAGE
- 1 CARROT
- ½ RED ONION
- 40 G SUGAR
- 1½ TBSP WHITE WINE VINEGAR
- 60 G SOUR CREAM
- 2 TSP WHOLEGRAIN MUSTARD
- 60 G NATURAL YOGHURT
- A COUPLE OF PINCHES OF SALT
- SMALL PINCH OF PEPPER

TO SERVE:
- ½ A BUNCH OF CHIVES, CHOPPED

Prep the veg by removing the core and outer leaves from the cabbage. In a food processor, shred the cabbage, the red onion and the carrots.

In a bowl, add the sugar, the white wine vinegar, the sour cream, the mustard, the yoghurt, and the salt and pepper and mix well. Add the cabbage, the onion and the carrots in, and mix through. Cover and refrigerate until required. This is one of those sides that gets better with time, so if you're having a barbecue, make this the night before. To serve, mix through the chopped chives.

SIMON'S HOME-MADE STUFFING

• •

- 800 G OF BREADCRUMBS
- 450 G OF BUTTER
- 3 LARGE WHITE ONIONS
- 50 G FRESH PARSLEY
- 50 G FRESH SAGE
- 50 G FRESH THYME
- SALT AND PEPPER TO SEASON
- 450 G OF PORK SAUSAGE MEAT

In a large bowl, add the breadcrumbs and the butter. Leave the butter out overnight, so it's easier to mix through the breadcrumbs. Mix together. Then finely dice the onions and the herbs, and add to the breadcrumb mixture and combine well. Add the sausage meat, and then the salt and pepper to season. Form the mixture into a large ball. This quantity will do you for about 5 portions, so break the large ball into 5 smaller balls, wrap them in Clingfilm and freeze until required. You can use this mixture to stuff a chicken for your Sunday roast etc. To use the stuffing straight away (for the Pilgrim sandwich for example) pop the stuffing into a frying pan, with a glug of olive oil and a knob of butter, and fry gently over a medium heat for about 10 to 15 mins. Let the stuffing cool, and then add to the sandwich!

ACKNOWLEDGEMENTS

ACKNOWLEDGEMENTS

===

I know it sounds like a cliché, but this book would not be in front of you right now without the Trojan work of a lot people. This is my opportunity to thank them all.

So let's start at the beginning of this book's journey, and that was with Simon and Declan at Gill Hess in Dublin (thank you, Stuart O'Connor, for the introduction!). These were the guys who I met first when the idea of a book was brewing. They immediately came on board and put me in touch with my now publishers, Black & White Publishing in Edinburgh. A huge thank you to Black & White, who had the belief in me and this project, and took the risk in offering me the opportunity to write this book. I truly hope you guys are happy with the end result. I know I am.

A huge thank you to my food guru, my right-hand man, my friend and all-round good-egg Neal Kearns. Neal has been on this journey with me since I signed up to take part in *Celebrity MasterChef*, guiding me through the series, and since then guiding me through a myriad of recipes that I wanted to appear in this book. Neal has gone above and beyond the call of duty, helping me write and rewrite all of these recipes, testing dishes, arranging all of the food for the photography, and basically opening his kitchen to me. On that note, a huge thank you to Guy Thompson, general manager at the Castleknock Hotel, who, along with Neal, gave me the facilities and support to get through *MasterChef*, and to write this book. The whole team over at the hotel welcomed me with open arms. Andrew (the cocktail king) and Bernie (always there with a cuppa and a smile), to name a couple, couldn't have done more for me. I am eternally grateful to all of the staff there.

One of the most important things to get right with this book was the photography. It was, according to my publishers, 'crucial' that we get the right person. And we did. I was so lucky to have found a quite brilliant photographer, Sean Cahill. Sean was recommended to us, and we arranged to get all of the photography done over the space of a week, in the hotel in Castleknock. I'd never met Sean before, but thirty minutes into our first day of shooting, I knew he was the man for the job. Straight away he created a 'look' for the dishes in the book, and worked so hard that week, with limited time (and props), and created beautiful shots. Sean, you are that rarest of gems, hard-working and incredibly creative. I'll skip over the bit about you being a vegetarian and subjecting you to photographing plates of meat for a week. But you did it with a smile. Thank you, Sean, you're a legend.

To all of those friends, family members and colleagues who I sent recipes to so they could test them for me, thank you so much! Your advice, feedback and support were vital to me in putting this book together. You are too many to name, but I promised I'd try, so thanks to Lorraine and Linda in LBM; all of the gang on weekend AM in TV3, Anna, Tommy, Laura, Ian, Jody, Billy, Brian, Philippa, Shannon; to the gang in the production office of *Don't Let Go* in Galway, Emer and Lorraine; to my sisters Sarah and Debbie, my brother David, to my sister-in-law Karen, and my mother-in-law Evelyn, I say thank you.

A big thanks, as always, to my agent, Lorraine Brennan. I've been lucky to have the same agent since day one, seventeen years ago. Lorraine has become one of my closest friends, a confidante, and the main reason that my family have been able to eat meals over those years. No one in the world works harder for me, and no one in the world appreciates the hours you put in on my behalf, Lorraine, than me. Thanks L'Oréal. (I call her L'Oréal because she's worth it. I'll get my coat . . .)

To have a two-Michelin-starred chef write the foreword for my first cookbook was a dream come true. Daniel Clifford has been a huge supporter of mine since we met on *MasterChef*, and I've had the pleasure of cooking alongside him at the Taste of Dublin event, which was an afternoon I'll never forget. I'm proud to call Daniel a friend. Thanks, pal.

Another person who has championed my food journey is the darling of the Irish food scene, Neven Maguire. Neven got in touch with me while he was watching *MasterChef*, and we exchanged texts, then met for a cuppa and have been friends since. He completely put his arms around my idea of this book, and has gone to great lengths to make sure that it happened. Neven arranged me for to cook demos at a number of food festivals around Ireland, festivals that I enjoyed immensely, and all in the company of Neven and his amazing brother Kenny. Lads, thank you so much for the help and support. You guys are rock stars with frying pans.

A mention too to my business partners and great friends Conor & Hugh McAllister, the dynamic brothers behind the hugely successful chain 'The Grafton Barber'. The lads have backed me from day one in my business ventures, and I'm so grateful to have them on my team. And speaking of my team, a huge thanks to Paul O'Connell, my right-hand man, who runs ALL of my social media platforms. Not a great rugby player, but a dab hand at Instagram!

And last, but by no means least, to my rock, and the love of my life, Lisa. My chief recipe-tester, taster, sous-chef, and my best friend. Lisa has never told me that I couldn't do anything. No matter how bizarre the flea-brained idea I come up with, be it for a business idea, a script, or a recipe, she'll support me. She'll say, 'Go for it.' And on the flip side, she's the one that's always there to pick up the pieces if it fails, and believe me there have been more failures than successes! And she does it all without question. She's given me a beautiful family, my boys Cameron, Elliot, Isaac and Lewis. The jewels in my crown, my reasons for everything I do. Thank you, Lisa. I love you.

And finally, thank you to you, the reader. Thank you for coming on this journey with me. In the words of Karen Carpenter, 'we've only just begun . . .'

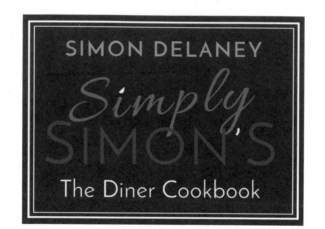

SIMON DELANEY

Simply

SIMON'S

The Diner Cookbook

twitter.com/simplysimonstv

facebook.com/simplysimonstv